The 1788 Morristown
GHOST HOAX

The Search for Lost Revolutionary War Treasure

PETER ZABLOCKI

THE
History
PRESS

Published by The History Press
Charleston, SC
www.historypress.com

First published 2022

Manufactured in the United States

ISBN 9781467150972

Library of Congress Control Number: 2022935413

Notice: The information in this book is true and complete to the best of our knowledge. It is offered without guarantee on the part of the author or The History Press. The author and The History Press disclaim all liability in connection with the use of this book.

For Igor.

Thank you for always supporting me, fighting the battles I could not fight for myself and knowing when to step back and let me figure out that I could.

—P.Z.

CONTENTS

PREFACE

Perhaps the inspiration for this book is found in the words of James West Davidson and Mark Hamilton Lytle, the authors of the bestselling *After the Fact: The Art of Historical Detection*, first published in 1982. In it, the two well-respected historians wrote:

> *This book began as an attempt to bring more life to the reading and learning of history. As young historians, we have been troubled by a growing disinterest in or even animosity toward the study of the past. How is it that when we and other historians have found so much that excited curiosity, other people find history irrelevant and boring? Perhaps, we thought, if lay readers and students understood better how historians go about their work—how they examine evidence, how they pose questions, and how they reach answers—history would engage them as it does us.*[1]

As a high school teacher for nearly two decades, it has been my career goal to make history more meaningful to my students, to have them understand that it is more than just a collection of facts and dates. As Historian E.H. Carr stated in his monumental and inspirational work *What Is History?*, "Historians…expect their work to be superseded again and again."[2] Namely, the stories we have of the past made their way down to our current generation through multiple minds that analyzed and evaluated them for their retelling. They no longer consist of "elemental and impersonal atoms, which nothing can alter."[3]

Sometimes, however, a story is deliberately shrouded in mystery from its onset. As there is not much to interpret, future historians stick to their retellings of the same tale. They alter some minor details here and there, but as there is not much to work with in the first place, the stories simply fall out of the consciousness of subsequent historians. When this happens, the stories revert back to the status of a nonhistorical fact and eventually become lost to posterity—or, as is the case with the story of the Morristown Ghost, they may become a caricature of themselves. They lose their historical context, the very historical fact that forms their basis. They turn into fables, tales told to kids around the campfire. They stop being history.

E.H. Carr discussed the process historians go through to "create history." To him, history began with the collection of known facts available to historians in documents, inscriptions and so on, "like fish on a fishmonger's slab." The historian then collects these facts, "takes them home and cooks and serves them in whatever style appeals to him."[4] Carr asserted that facts do not speak for themselves; they only speak when a historian calls on them. It is the historian who decides which facts to give spotlight to and in what order and context to give them. "It is the historian who has decided for his own reasons that Caesar's crossing of that petty stream, the Rubicon, is a fact of history, whereas the crossing of the Rubicon by millions of other people before or since interests nobody at all."[5] The famous historian maintained that "the fact that you arrived in this building half an hour ago on foot, or on a bicycle, or in a car, is just as much a fact about the past as the fact that Caesar crossed the Rubicon…but it will probably be ignored by historians." Thus, history comes to us through the selection process and the subsequent analysis of empirical facts collected by historians.

One would assume that if the building blocks of history, the so-called facts, are "pure," so is the historian's process of creating history. Yet, as Carr also pointed out, "the facts never come to us 'pure,' since they do not and cannot exist in pure form: they are always refracted through the mind of the recorder. It follows that when we take up a work of history, our first concern should be not with the facts which it contains but with the historian who wrote it [and the context they wrote it in.]"[6] What if only one artifact of that given time exists to detail the story in question, as is the case with the story of the Morristown Ghost? And what if the author of the work is also unknown?

Furthermore, what if there is not a plethora of accounts, diary entries or even names associated with the event? At that point, the historian's selection process is already done. History did not leave them with much in terms of initial facts on the case, thus all they have to work with is already someone's single interpretation of the event. And perhaps more importantly, there is no way to corroborate said account with another, as none other detailing it exists. This turn of events best describes the work that you hold in your hands. One can quickly look up the tale of the Morristown Ghost in various collections and compilations of New Jersey's ghost stories, legends and folklores. The account appears alongside the more well-known New Jersey Devil. The latter was designed in 1938 as the country's only state demon, described as a "kangaroo-like creature with the face of a horse, the head of a dog, bat-like wings, horns and a tail."[7] Like the state's devil, the Morristown Ghost is no longer what it once was, history grounded in fact.

The work you hold in your hands attempts to draw the story of the Morristown Ghost out of the folklore basement, where it has been relegated over the past few centuries. Perhaps by dragging it out of the realm of fiction and placing it back into historical fact and context, we can add to the already rich history of the state of New Jersey. According to E.H. Carr, the best way to do this is to not concern ourselves so much with what it says but focus on where it fits in historical context and why its author would choose to shroud it in mystery from its onset. What follows is a narrative based in facts—or a single pamphlet that initially detailed the event—and the historical process of detection that attempts to place the tale in a historical framework. The hope is that people of all ages can get as excited about studying the past as we historians do each time we try to place ourselves—or, for lack of a better word, lose ourselves—in history's narrative. Returning to James West Davidson and Mark Hamilton Lytle:

> *History is not something that is simply brought out of the archives, dusted off and displayed as "the way things really were." It is a painstaking construction, held together only with the help of assumptions, hypothesis and inferences. Readers of history who push dutifully onward, unaware of the backstage work, miss the essence of the discipline. They miss the opportunity to question and to judge their reading critically. Most of all, they miss the chance to learn how enjoyable it can be to go out and do a bit of digging themselves.*

So how real is the story of the Morristown Ghost? On one hand, it is very real indeed. Yet on the other, it is not real at all. In fact, it is not even a ghost story. However, it is a snapshot of a state and its people ravaged by war and years of prejudice against each other. It is a story of human greed, a tale of blind superstitions and a people's inability to get past them. It's the story of a town seeking to redeem itself from the label of being a backward society, one unable to look to the future by clinging to the past. And in the middle of it all, it is a story of a great con, the Morristown Con of 1788.

Peter Zablocki
Denville, New Jersey (five miles outside of Morristown)
October 25, 2020

ACKNOWLEDGEMENTS

Not much would have happened with relation to this book if not for the help of Kat Kurylko, a research assistant at the Morris County Historical Society. Thank you for being so helpful with this research and allowing me to examine the Morristown Ghost files collected by the county over the years. Similarly, thank you to Tim Cutler of Digital Antiquaria for sharing his files and resources with me.

A great thank-you has to also go out to Michael Dolan of the *American History* magazine, who has taken the time to help me become a better writer and historian through his constant feedback and opportunities. Also, a sincere thank-you to Mr. James West Davidson for his words of encouragement, advice and simply for taking the time to converse with a very humbled historian. A thank-you also goes out to Danielle Elia, Dr. Steve Racine, Heather Pollak and Matt Arroyo for their continual words of support and encouragement. And last but not least, I'd like to say a great thank-you to the two people who never let me forget to stay grounded, Tom Reszka and Oliver Efremoski.

INTRODUCTION

In a village near Morristown (presumably today's Chatham, New Jersey), 1789.

A group of around twenty men sat quietly in a dark room. The sweat was dripping off their brows. They could all smell the heavy aroma of hard cider in the air, knowing that perhaps they might have had too much to drink that night. The burning candles seemed to add to the unbearable heat but were necessary to provide the little light they did. The "Company," as they called themselves—all faces in the dark shadows—stood quietly, looking at the man at the head of the little round table in the center of the parlor. In fact, they were the who's who of the local community—lawyers, an eminent jurist, two justices of the peace, two doctors and a retired colonel—all wealthy landowners. It was a small room. They felt crowded, yet no one dared to complain or even speak for that matter. If all went the way it should, unspeakable riches would soon be theirs for the taking.

Then the house came alive. With the first groans coming from the hallway, the men snapped to attention. Before they could turn toward the door, the windows rattled. The sounds of jingling coins, nails scratching at walls and hard knocks on floorboards seemed to come from every direction. Suddenly, as if from directly behind the man sitting at the small table—the presumed leader of the group—came a shrieking voice. "Look to God!" Genuinely afraid, the men did as they were told before the meeting began. They fell on their knees and prayed. After what seemed like an eternity, the Company stood up and walked alternately around the room five times, in silence. Fear gripped them as the floorboards creaked under their heavy feet. No one spoke. Some whimpered; others sniffled. They all continued the predetermined ritual. No one thought to look at the smirking man sitting at the table in the middle of the room. Perhaps it was too dark to see his face anyway. Still, Ransford Rogers knew he had them exactly where he wanted them.

New Jersey—Morris County to be specific—has a vibrant history. Historians consider it to have been the military capital of the American Revolution. Because of its strategic location, General George Washington chose it as the winter encampment for his Continental army not once but twice during the duration of the conflict. Yet Morristown, the city center and de facto capital of the county, badly ravished by the war, was not immune to its share of scandals, and its upper-class citizenry was not quite done with taking abuse. Since the town's population discovered, pursued and aided in the capture of Samuel Ford, a leader of a notorious gang of counterfeiters shortly before the war, it is that much more shocking to discover that the same population was conned once again just a few years later, this time handing over a sum of roughly $40,000 in today's money. The benefactor of the 1788 ploy? A ghost, the "Morristown Ghost" to be precise.

In the late 1700s, a booklet titled *The Morristown Ghost: An Account of the Beginning, Transactions, and Discovery of Ransford Rogers, Who Seduced Many by Pretend Hobgoblins and Apparitions, and Thereby Extorted Money from Their Pockets in the County of Morris and State of New Jersey, in the Year of 1788* appeared. The author of the work is not known. Over the years, there has been some speculation about who put pen to paper to uncover a story that many known members of the community would have loved to remain hidden forever. Some believe that the book's author was the con artist himself, Ransford Rogers, who wanted to punish and further embarrass the Morristown people, who he felt had done him wrong. Others, on account of the paper and print similarity to then published *New Jersey Journal*, believe the pamphlet was the work of newspaper editor Sheppard Kollock of Elizabethtown. There might be some truth to the assertion, as Sheppard had the means and the background to make such a work readily available to the masses. His newspaper peaked in popularity in the late 1780s and was the state's leading source of Revolutionary War news and events. The information for

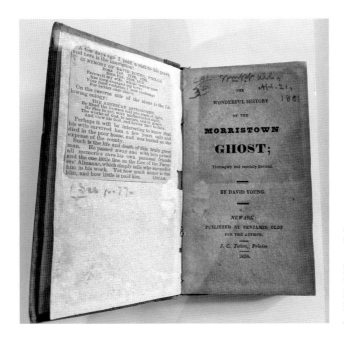

An original copy of the David Young 1826 *Morristown Ghost* pamphlet located at the Morris County Historical Society in Morristown. *Photograph by the author.*

the paper was sometimes directly supplied by George Washington himself. As for the impetus for the publication of a work that would shame so many prominent people for being "duped" by a ghost story, there is no clear explanation. To this day, we cannot say with any certainty who authored the controversial pamphlet.

Upon its initial publication in 1792, the work was actively sought out and destroyed by the families who managed to get swindled by Rogers. They were successful to the extent that by the 1820s, not a single copy was known to have survived. Around this time, David "Philom" Young, the famous founder of *The Farmers' Almanac*, accidentally found one last known copy of the pamphlet while visiting a friend in Elizabeth, New Jersey. The story was too good to pass over. The eccentric schoolmaster, mathematician and author published his own version in 1826, *The Wonderful History of the Morristown Ghost; Thoroughly and Carefully Revised.* The new publication, as well as the initial affair on which it was based, caused quite a stir in the town of Morristown, as many of the families involved still resided in the vicinity and did not want the stories of their parents and grandparents being associated with crude superstitions, a basic lack of common sense and the tendency to be gullible. In fact, when writing the official *History of Morris County* in 1882 and the multivolume history of *Northwestern New Jersey*, edited by A. Van Doren Honeyman in 1927, the authors of both works, just as Young did, omitted the last names of those involved in order to prevent any further unpleasantries for the families' descendants. Also noted is the fact that by the time a facsimile copy of the original history was being compiled and published by L.A. and B.H. Voght in 1887, an authentic original copy of the 1792 work—apart from Young's alleged copy—had still not been found.

The following is an account of perhaps the greatest, silliest and most naïve con in one of the most historically significant counties in the annals of American history. One might say that the story began in the summer of 1788, when two Morris County men, while traveling through Smith's Clove, New York, fell in with a schoolteacher from Connecticut, one Ransford Rogers. Yet perhaps a better starting point might be the 1770s, when known Morristown Loyalists, seeing the futility in the British Crown's ability to hold onto its colonies, presumably decided to bury their treasure before it was plundered and seized for the Patriot cause. The rest reads like a fable, a legend of sorts; yet in this case, it is nothing short of a fact. Looking through the literature on the subject, it quickly becomes evident that history dismissed the story as a folktale. While the tale of Rogers, the Schooley's Mountain treasure and the Morristown Ghost has appeared in various collections of the state's ghost stories, its placement is flawed, as is its delivery. Also, the average length of the legend never goes beyond a few pages within a larger context of the state's supernatural occurrences.

The purpose of the research you hold in your hands is to examine the event for what it was, a swindle, a scam or, for lack of a better word, a con. Most certainly, it is not a ghost legend. Relying heavily on the original pamphlet and various histories and accounts from the time and the area, we gain a better understanding of the event by placing it into a greater historical context. The probability of the treasure's existence, the belief in the supernatural and the likelihood of a con of such magnitude being pulled off are all examined and analyzed in this book in detail. Taking it all into account, it becomes very obvious that the period directly after the Revolutionary War in the state of New Jersey created a perfect setting—if there ever was any—for the events that grace these pages to take place. The details bring to light the psychological, social and economic contexts of the local history of post–American Revolution Morris County.

The state, often referred to as the "Cockpit of the Revolution," was pillaged by the Continental and British armies alike, and many farms were left destroyed. Morris County, and Morristown specifically, were securely landlocked directly in the middle of the action, both literately and figuratively speaking. The village of Morristown was located between the Delaware and

Hudson Rivers in the center of northern New Jersey, thirty miles west of New York City and seventy-five miles northeast of Philadelphia. It was also approximately the same distance from the three main British ports in New Jersey at New Brunswick, Newark and Perth Amboy.[8] Thus, the scars and desperation left over from the war might explain why few individuals in the area would have ignored the promise of a better life. With poverty rampant, the hopes of making a quick buck sure seemed enthralling.

Subsequently, many people from the area found themselves displaced because of their Loyalist beliefs toward Britain, further causing strife between them and the other townspeople. This became the basis of the belief that those same people could never have possibly taken all their possessions with them on the run and hence must have hidden them somewhere. The story of the actual Loyalists of Morris County, as well as their riches, is far from a simple narrative. We gain a better appreciation for the feasibility of the existence of a Schooley's Mountain treasure when we place it within the context of people's treatment, their hasty removal and the confiscation of their property.

As for the belief in the supernatural, the state of New Jersey was far from immune to the superstitions of the time. The most considerable evidence of this were the Mount Holly witch trials, which were reported in the

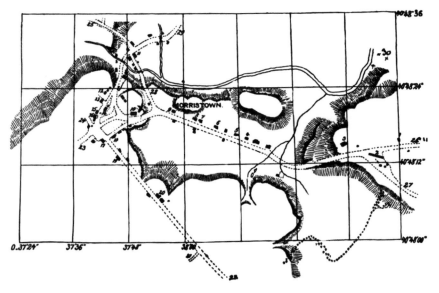

A plan of Morristown by a survey ordered by General Washington in 1777. *Courtesy of the Morris County Historical Society.*

Pennsylvania Gazette on October 22, 1730—more on that later. Supposedly, around three hundred people gathered "to see the experiment or two tried on some persons accused of witchcraft."[9] In fact, Quaker Pennsylvania and New Jersey were more multicultural than other colonies and held numerous witch trials during the 1700s. Luckily, none led to executions ordered by the courts. There were, however, riots in which suspected witches were killed by mobs as late as 1787, a year before the events of the Morristown Ghost.[10] According to Mount Vernon (George Washington's estate) historians, who researched colonial superstitions at the time of George Washington's political career, what was far more common in this area was a belief in spiritualism. There are accounts of people attempting to communicate with the dead or resurrect their bodies, as there was a strong belief that the Holy Spirit had the power to heal people.[11] And while there were more people who knew better than to believe in the supernatural or magic as a whole, there were those among them who still believed. Considering the facts, it becomes less remarkable that the people of Morristown believed in witches and hobgoblins.

And then there is the con itself. Colonial New Jersey was not a safe haven by any means. With theft being the most prevalent crime committed, crime rates pushed the state to create the first state prison in New Jersey on March 1, 1797.[12] Furthermore, in accordance with the state's criminal codes, enacted in 1668 and 1675 and modified but still present at the time of the event, practicing witchcraft was on par with committing murder, perjury, sodomy, abduction or rape—an offense punishable with jail time at minimum and the death penalty at maximum.[13] While the stringent laws and the death penalty were curtailed significantly by new decrees in December 1761, witchcraft remained a vice punishable by law. As the small settlements were becoming small towns with growing wealth and land acquisitions, protecting one's property took center stage in determining what constituted criminal activity. The theft of property, including burglary and robbery, became the most prevalent offense committed. Forgery, counterfeiting currency and picking pockets, along with other forms of petty thefts, took center stage in the Morris County area at the time.[14] By 1788, the town could add deception, deceit, racket, blackmail and a ghost scam to the list of crimes committed within its borders. Unfortunately, those involved were too embarrassed to make the scam enough of an issue to have it officially go down in history as a crime—until now, that is.

PART I

THE MORRISTOWN GHOST

1

THE MORRISTOWN GHOST

The following narrative of events pertaining to the Morristown Ghost presents the facts as recorded in the original pamphlet of 1792, The Wonderful Story of the Morristown Ghost *of 1826 and* Fac-Simile Copy *of the* Morristown Ghost *of 1876. All quoted text comes from the original pamphlets. The conversations are given as they appeared, and they were corroborated by the cited sources unless specified with brackets.*

The two Morris County men were far from home. It was the early summer of 1788, and searching for mining work had led the two young men to Smith's Clove in the state of New York. Although Morris County was not the initial impetus for their journey, the travelers carried a well-known secret that had baffled their Morris County, New Jersey neighbors. It was a common belief in their hometown that large amounts of gold and silver were buried in Morristown throughout the Revolutionary War. Although only five years had passed since the war's end, many had tried but none succeeded in locating the treasure. Supposedly buried at Schooley's Mountain by British Loyalists as a means of concealment from confiscation by Patriot colonists, the fortune eluded all those who set out to find it. It did not take long for those seeking the bounty to excuse their bad luck by claiming that the set loot was bewitched and protected by spirits. The two men who set out on their travels even heard some say that the bodies of murdered Loyalists were purposefully buried along with the gold to become its eternal protectors. Since the pair's arrival in New England, their search for work proved fruitless, yet the two young men would not allow themselves to be disheartened. It would all be worth it if they could only find someone who possessed the art of dispelling spirits. They knew of the stories told by the elder folk back home—stories of witches and warlocks capable of such powers. Apparently, another drifter seeking to find his way in a ravaged postwar landscape of a new nation also knew of these stories.

Ransford Rogers of Connecticut was a schoolteacher by trade. While some accounts describe him as illiterate, that notion can be dismissed by the fact that history places him in three different schoolhouses in three different states as a teacher of young children. The young man "had the power of inspiring confidence…was very affable in his manners and had a genius adequate to prepossess people in his favor." He was also described as being "very ambitious to maintain an appearance of possessing profound knowledge." In other words, he was a perfect con artist. The Morris County travelers came across Rogers by chance while passing by his schoolhouse in Smith's Clove. Striking up a conversation with the man, the tired travelers were invited to stay the night. By early dawn, they were convinced that they had found the right man to help them dig up something much greater than what they would encounter on their mining journey into the nation's heartland.

The coffee was warm as the young men described the story of the mountain treasure. Rogers did not interrupt them but simply nodded and made approving gestures. "[We need] someone whose knowledge descends into the bowels of the earth and who could reveal the secret things of darkness," they proclaimed. Ransford, seeing an opportunity, expressed to them that they need not seek any further. He possessed a "deep knowledge of chemistry" and the sciences, he claimed. This knowledge, which he acquired through his travels, had given him the power to raise and dispel good or evil spirits. The two men looked at each other; they agreed without having to say anything. Rogers needed to come back with them to Morristown, New Jersey. There would be no more searching for work in their future.

Playing his part masterfully, Rogers was not quick to agree. With the excitement hidden behind his stern face, his mind was quickly working out a plan. He could not leave, he told the two men, as being a schoolteacher was his true calling. Through assurances of the possibility of opening a school, Ransford Rogers finally agreed to accompany the men back to Morris County, New Jersey. Upon their arrival in Morristown in August 1788, young Rogers's reputation as an educator was quickly validated by locals who had recently come into some wealth after the war and desired a proper education for their children. According to *Northwestern New Jersey: A History*, written in 1927, Ransford was hired as a schoolteacher in a schoolhouse on

Mendham Road, three miles outside of the village of Morristown, today's town of Chester, New Jersey. Each night after his students left for the day, the mysterious newcomer was seen on his horse galloping toward Morristown's Schooley's Mountain. One night in early September, while sitting on his horse watching the sun go down behind the trees on the mountain, the young man concluded that the opportunity that had presented itself to him was perhaps too great for him to take advantage of alone. The next day, Rogers asked the townsfolk for some time off to travel to his hometown in New England to see some of his ailing family. He returned by the end of the month with his main accomplice, whom he hid in plain sight as simply another drifter who had found his way into town. Ironically named Mr. Goodenough, the associate would not allow himself to be seen with Rogers so as not to raise any suspicions. The men were ready; it was finally time to set the wheels of their plan in motion.

The two young men who initiated the quest for the supernatural treasure hunt were allowed to seek out other like-minded individuals interested in acquiring Mr. Rogers's services. Apart from the travelers, the rest of the people brought into the secret circle were honorable members of Morristown society. Totaling eight men, the group convened in Rogers's home in a most secret meeting. Speaking in a calm voice, the young teacher "communicated to them the solemnity of the business and the intricacy of the undertaking." The young travelers, excited to be in the company of such known townsfolk, could not stop smiling. For sure, they would not only be rewarded with treasure but would also forever be known as the ones who aided in the treasure's reveal through contracting with the young Rogers. Yet even their smiles soon faded, replaced with anxiety and apprehension. "There had been several persons murdered and buried with the money to retain it in the earth," exclaimed Ransford. These spirits needed to be drawn out and spoken to before any money could be gathered. "[I can] by [my] art and power raise these apparitions, and the whole company might hear [me] converse with them and satisfy themselves there [is] no deception." At that very moment, a noise was heard directly outside the room's only window. The men jumped up quickly, yet they were just slow enough to miss seeing Mr. Goodenough outside, hurrying away with a masked object and a hammer in his hand. Before departing, the teacher warned his followers to "refrain from all immorality, lest the spirits should be provoked and withhold the treasure."

Ransford knew that the group's members, transfixed by dreams of riches, would communicate their hopes to their friends. As a matter of fact, he hoped

Ruins of the old ironworks on Speedwell Avenue between Morris Plains and Morristown, where Ransford was known to operate during his con. *Photograph by the author.*

that they would. Still, with a larger group, the secret of his actions needed to be secure. He needed the men to go beyond just believing. He needed them to be afraid. The members, who came to call themselves the "Fire Club," or simply the "Company," grew to the size of some forty men. While they met secretly in their homes, plotting what they would do with their riches, Rogers constantly updated them on the progress. For days at a time, young Ransford would hold meetings with the spirits, acting as a go-between. And each day, the man would play up his role by making himself look spent, tired and even scared. This particular morning, however, he really was tired.

The schoolteacher raised his hand to quiet his accomplice. It was dark on Schooley's Mountain, and although they were surrounded by trees, Ransford could not risk being caught by a stray rider. Assured by Mr. Goodenough that they were alone, Ransford returned to digging holes spread out around the mountain. It was early in the night. It would take a few hours for his chemical traps to activate. This was perfect, as it needed to be dark for their maximum effect. The chemical brew, a concoction of crude gunpowder, "would break and cause great explosions, which appeared dismal in the night and would cause great timidity." By the morning hours, some families in the area awoke to blasts and smoke appearing out of the ground without a soul around to set them off. At least a few individuals witnessed the commotion, making it the talk of the town. That night, Rogers held a meeting with the Company, letting them know that he was close to convincing the spirits to reveal themselves to them. In a few days, they would visit the mountain together.

The rain would not let up, and thunder could be heard for miles as the men from the Company rode—some eight and others even twelve miles—from all over Morris County to the predetermined location in the hills of Morristown. They knew that many a man had died from contracting sicknesses caused by being out in such unfavorable weather, but still, every man was punctual in his attendance. Rogers could not be happier with Mr. Goodenough's performance. Upon their arrival, the men were met with random explosions that seemed to appear out of thin air. They were small enough to not be heard outside the vicinity of the mountain, but still, they were large enough to frighten all those in attendance. From under the brims of their wet hats, the members of the Company noticed an elaborate system of paths—circular, elliptical, square and serpentine—carved into the earth. "A thousand men could not have performed such a task," lamented one individual. "[These had to have been made by] demoniac powers," added another. Mr. Goodenough had indeed played his part masterfully. A "thousand men," thought Rogers—if they only knew. Not letting his guard down, Rogers continued to play his role of a caring yet surprised and nervous leader.

A noise came from behind distant trees, a voice, distorted, beckoning Rogers to come forward. Standing in awe, the men watched their leader walk behind the trees. At this time, more of the earlier-buried chemicals erupted, further adding to the eeriness of the situation. Frozen in place, the men could barely hear the conversation between the schoolteacher and the spirit. In reality, the man's accomplice was speaking through what was later presumed to have been an apparatus of some kind. "[The men] must meet on an appointed night in a field half a mile from any house, where they must form certain angles and circles," the men heard the spirit say before being interrupted by thunder. As Ransford finished his conversation and walked back through the muddy dirt to his followers, he informed them that the spirit had added that if they did not do as he said and remained inside their circles' boundaries, the evil spirits would punish them. Until further notice, only Rogers was permitted to speak with the ghost. Looking into their faces as they mounted their horses to ride back to their farms, Ransford Rogers knew there were no longer any skeptics among them.

The leaves were nearly all on the ground in late November 1788, when the Company convened in the field near a village in Morris County. As the men began arriving, they quietly joined the procession already within the circle. There was scarce lighting, as only a few candles were present around the large circle that had been prepared before their arrival. The candles cast "a ghastly, melancholy, direful gloom through the [surrounding] woods." It was ten o'clock at night, and they all knew why they were there. This was going to be the day that they would become wealthy.

On one part of the circle, four posts were erected on which to spread a cloth. This formed a tent, from under which Rogers then looked upon his disciples. He watched in silence as about forty men walked in front of him alternatively around the circle. "After they had been rotating…for a considerable amount of time with great decorum, they were instantaneously shocked with the most impetuous explosion from the earth at a small distance from them." Many jumped, and some even fainted as the previously compounded hidden substance illuminated the night sky. The flames rising at a considerable height brought to light the frightening atmosphere among the Company and "presented many dreadful objects from the supposed haunted grove, which was instantaneously involved in obscurity." Then came the loud groans and the same raspy voice from behind the tent, beckoning Ransford to walk toward the woods. Afraid to leave the circle, the men watched in terror as their leader got up and left the tent to discourse with the spirits.

Just as in all of their previous meetings, the men could hardly make out what was said. "We have the possessions of a vast fortune and cannot give it up unless we proceed regular and without variance; and as fortune had discriminated you to receive the treasure, [in good faith], you must deliver to us, every man, twelve pounds." No treasure could be disclosed unless the money was paid in gold and silver. The spirits then pressed on with explaining that they would only communicate with Rogers. He would be the "conductor." In turn, the Company had to adhere to his precepts and do as he said. "We know all things and will detect the man that attempts to defraud his neighbor." As Rogers returned to his tent, he was met with faces that then undoubtedly looked to him for protection from the spirits' potential wrath, especially if they failed to procure their peace offerings.

It was three o'clock in the morning when all men rode out for home, pondering how they would come up with the required sum of money. Backing out now meant that the anger of the supernatural would befall

The corner of the Backing Ridge and New Vernon Roads, three miles south of the Morristown Green. This is what the area around Morristown looked like during the event of the Morristown Ghost. *Courtesy of the Morris County Historical Society.*

them. The only man who could protect them was a one-time teacher from Connecticut. To them, the hobgoblins and apparitions were real, and Rogers was more than a mere man. Some would later say that his influence was beyond question, and if "he put one of [us] to death, he would have been justified and defended by the rest."[15] Because not everyone could afford the twelve pounds, Ransford told those in need that half of the amount would suffice and that he would procure the remainder. Subsequently, the next few meetings at the schoolteacher's home dealt with the Company's progress of acquiring the desired sums. Each night, Rogers told the men of his communications with the spirits, and each night, Mr. Goodenough played his part splendidly, making eerie sounds in and around the house. By December, when the Company was slow in coming up with the money, the apparition spoke to the men gathered in Rogers's room once more. "Press forward!" said the raspy voice. "We were sent to deliver [your] society great riches and will not rest until [we] had given it up; but the money [we] request is only an acknowledgment for such immense treasures."

What caused members of the Company many sleepless nights was the request from the spirit for the money to be paid in specie, namely silver or gold. It had only been a few years since the end of the Revolutionary War, and the state of New Jersey was still trying to find its way. Like the rest of the nation under the Articles of Confederation, the most accessible currency in the state was loan paper, not gold or silver. If obtained in New Jersey, specific currency would be worthless if Ransford attempted to escape to any other state. Rogers continued to press his advantage. Already scared, the men were called upon to meet at his home nearly every night throughout the winter. As it was often impossible to acquire the gold, many mortgaged their farms and disposed of their cattle at half price rather than fail to obtain the required sum. Surprisingly, their neighbors were not curious enough to ask any questions. The men were sworn to secrecy. If they brought too much attention to their deeds and were exposed, they could lose their lives or the lives of those dear to them. Rogers took his time—after all, the only good con was the one he could get away with. He also held his ground when it came to the gold and silver.

It was March 1789 when Ransford and Mr. Goodenough thought they had secured enough money. Yet fearing that something might happen that would break the con they had so elaborately built up, the teacher decided to take it a step further. For the next few weeks, Ransford, using the same apparatus to conceal his voice, visited some of his disciples by standing outside their windows at night. He was always careful to warn them that coming too close to the window would result in a curse. Seeing themselves as lucky to have been chosen, the men who were visited by the spirit would convey the messages from these conversations at the required whole-group meetings. This would not only further legitimize Rogers but also stressed fortitude. Yet the flock was becoming too impatient. Many began to voice their displeasure; some were even willing to risk the hobgoblins' wrath and search Schooley's Mountain themselves. They were quickly reminded that many had tried and none had succeeded in the endeavor. Rogers could not risk the con falling apart, especially since he had come so far. Consequently, he convened the Company in April and informed them of the date they were all waiting for. The spirits had spoken. They were to meet at Schooley's Mountain on May 1, in a month.

Ransford Rogers took the whole month to prepare for his greatest spectacle yet. Some have alluded to the fact that he even hired more hands to carry out his great encore. If he did, the names of those who participated in the hoax that night have never been recorded, and like the spirits of Morristown, the confirmation of their very existence was also never found. The men gathered inside the already prepared circle and solemnly began to move within it. Once inside, it was forbidden to step out so as not to offend the spirits—they had come too far now to let a little lack of concentration take it all away. In a moment's time, two ghosts appeared some distance from the circle. "They exhibited symptoms of wreathing themselves [and slowly twisting in unnatural ways] into postures which appeared most ghastly in the darkness." Screeching and growling noises seemed to come from every direction. Then there was an explosion in the distance, followed by frightful screams coming from the woods. The trees seemed to close in on them, an apparition made more realistic through the smoke from various small explosions. The two ghosts seemed to multiply.

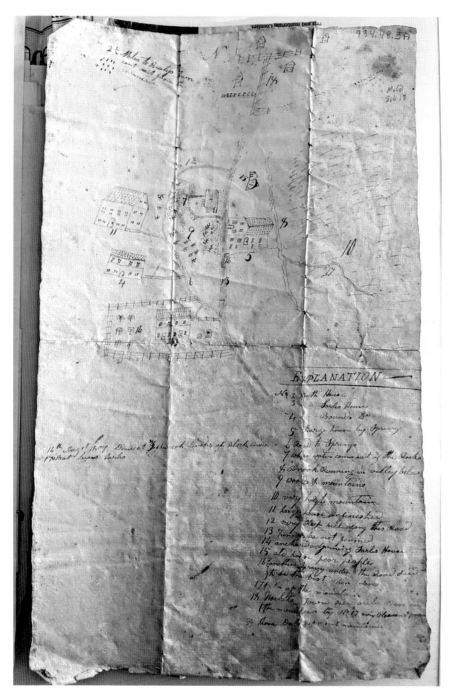

The hand-drawn map of Schooley's Mountain from 1809 is barely visible. *Courtesy of the Morris County Historical Society.*

Then the voice spoke once more. "You have not proceeded regularly; some of you were faithless, and several things were divulged which ought to have been kept profoundly secret. The wicked disposition of many of the company and your irregular proceedings had debarred you from receiving the treasures presently." Until Rogers stepped in and began to dispel the hobgoblins and apparitions in the name of God, the Company's punishment seemed imminent. This seemed to last a few moments as the Company's protector battled the spirits for their safety. As some of the grown men began to cry, the figures on the outskirts of the circle began to draw just close enough to remain mysterious shadows to those inside the circle. Yet they were too close for the men's comfort. Ransford continued yelling out his banishing words intertwined with prayers. There were more noises. The circle and the smoke seemed to close in on them even more. Then there was another loud explosion, louder than anything before it. And then all was quiet.

Rogers stood inside the circle with his followers. "He appeared as much frightened as the rest of them after being scarcely able to appease the spirits. Nobody spoke; they all knew that if it were not for the schoolteacher, they would no longer walk among the living. All thoughts of money were forgotten, and the members looked to Rogers only for protection." Nobody seemed to care when Rogers assured them that if the spirit came back to see him, he would notify them right away. With many still visibly shaken and some sobbing, the Company thanked Rogers wholeheartedly and mounted their horses.

Alone on a knoll, Ransford Rogers took a deep breath, sighed and turned to look at the ridgeline of Schooley's Mountain. He then waited and watched as Mr. Goodenough made his way up to the knoll. Congratulations were in order.

2

ROGERS'S NEW PROJECT

Had Ransford Rogers stopped and not continued another con, he would have been "feared and respected, and the capricious notions of witchcraft, hobgoblins and the devil would have prevailed among those deceived, with [much] prejudice, fear and ignorance." Yet he once again allowed himself to be influenced by others, this time by two young men from New England. Having resigned from his teaching post in the town near Morristown, Ransford moved into a larger home in Morristown proper. The summer of 1789 was ending, Mr. Goodenough had taken his share and ridden out of town, and Rogers was ready to retire—at least until he heard a knock on his door. Two young travelers from the north had heard that a fellow New Englander resided in these parts and hoped he would allow them to stay the night. Once inside by the fire, the two men disclosed to Ransford that they had heard of his great con back in New England. Was it his old accomplice who was too careless with his money and drew too much attention to himself back home? It did not matter to Rogers; he knew he did not have a choice once the travelers asked him to help them repeat his feat from the year prior. They could not go after the same men. Many of the original Company had licked their wounds and retreated to their farms, never having spoken about the long and eerie nights spent with Rogers. It seems like Ransford, having been used to a traveling lifestyle, should have simply snuck out at night with his wealth and moved on to another state. It is hard to say why he did not. Maybe it was the fear of disclosing to his new accomplices the place where he had hidden his treasure, the fear of being killed for it once he retrieved it or even his own rekindled desire for more riches that kept him in Morristown. No one knows for sure—except Ransford himself.

The men decided that this time, the new Company would not be made up of wealthy landowners. There was no need to draw too much attention. They would target quaint, honest and loyal church members. The ghosts and apparitions would have to appeal to the strong religious beliefs of the men in question. Since the Second Great Awakening was already in its early stages, the timing could not have been any more perfect. Characterized by peace, morality and a fervent belief in God on Earth, the movement was already having an effect on the eastern portions of the nation. People began to believe that it was their actions on earth that determined whether they would go to Heaven or Hell, and thus, it was up to them to oppose "the Devil"—or as would be seen in a few months' time, to fear him. The conspirators traveled within a twenty-mile radius in Morris County, visiting prominent churchgoers while planning their next scam. Once recruited, the members of the Company heard the tale of a "spirit of a just man" that had descended from the heavens to bless those in need and those in possession of a high spiritual love for God with the gifts of mortal riches.

It was an uncommonly cool July evening in 1789 when the new Company arrived at Rogers's Morristown home. Together with Ransford and the two New Englanders, the Company once again began with eight members. Skeptical at first, the new followers, along with others, began to walk around the room within a circle that had been painted on the floorboards and illuminated with candles held in place by melted wax. While they were performing this ceremony, various noises were heard around the house. It is unclear if Mr. Goodenough had returned to partake in this second project or if Ransford and his partners had employed someone else to assist them. Perhaps it was the partners who took on the "ghostly" duties. The men inside the circle stopped moving as the noises intensified. "There was the rattling of a wagon, groaning, striking upon the windows." Rogers spurred them on, "Don't stop!" The men were then directed to take a sheet of paper from a neat pile on the kitchen table. Wrapping the paper around their wrists, all the men, Ransford included, stepped outside the door of the home and into the night. With their eyes closed and arms out, they awaited the spirit to tell them how to proceed. "After holding them thus a considerable time, they withdrew them and, having previously huddled the papers together, examined them, when lo! On one was written a time when they were to convene and receive further directions from the spirit."[16] The paper, meticulously prepared by Ransford Rogers ahead of time, called for a new meeting a week from that day.

When the predetermined night arrived, both the con artists and those who were being deceived united in prayer as they knelt within a circle in the middle of the room. This time, the con was centered on Christian beliefs and thus took on a more of a "God versus the Devil" connotation. Upon completing the prayer, the men paraded around the room in a procession and in the order of their age from youngest to oldest. They did so eight times, once for each person in the room. Like last time, the men picked up a sheet of paper and proceeded outside the house, into a nearby field. As their eyesight adjusted, the Company could make out a circle presumably made up of small stones. The designated space was reported to have been about twelve feet in diameter. Once in the circle, the men fell on their knees and, pressing their faces to the ground, extended their arms, holding out their papers. Only with their eyes closed and through loud prayer could the Holy Ghost enter the circle to give its message. As the men were convinced that they were communicating with something no less than an angel, they dared not disobey any of its directions. "Amen!" screamed Rogers, "[You may stand up]." After marching back to the house, the Company unfolded their papers. As was usually the case, one man was the lucky recipient of the spirit's message.

"The Company must be increased by eleven members, and each one must deposit to the spirit the sum of twelve pounds of silver or gold." The gifts were meant to prove the Company's loyalty to the spirit. This proof would show the ghost that they were worthy of passing on a treasure it was tasked with holding onto until such a time seemed appropriate. It was also a means of proving their Christian faith and belief in God. While all the men marveled at the spirit's writing, not all believed in its message. In fact, as the men rode home that night, some resolved to quit the endeavor before it really got started. Ransford knew he had to act quickly if he was to hold onto his new con.

One night that week, Rogers covered himself in a sheet under a long coat and a low-sitting brimmed hat and visited a house of one of the doubting men. Luckily, he did not even need to worry about getting the man's attention, as his intended target was already outside. Catching the man off guard and utilizing the rigged voice-changing device, Ransford warned him not to turn around, lest great evil befell him. Not just any mere mortal could see the spirit, it said. He then related to him that he had vast treasure in his possession and that a company was in pursuit of it; he could not give it up unless some of the church members joined them. "I am the spirit of a just man, and I am first to give you information how to proceed and put the conducting of it into your hands; and I will be ever with you and give you directions when you go amiss; therefore, fear not, but go to Rogers and inform him of you interview with me—fear not, I am ever with you."[17] Early the next morning, Ransford acted in awe when he was informed of the delivery of his very own message. He would no longer be the conductor between the spirit and the Company. That honor was then bestowed on a well-respected church leader.

The new conductor then went on to recruit new members. His position in town most certainly worked in his favor. Many religious, humble and empathetic souls from his congregation agreed to join the man's secret quest to "help a spirit of a just man." The author of the original pamphlet did not know if the new members joined as a potential investment of seeing some of their money turn into an undisclosed treasure or for the simple sake of helping a fellow Christian or even solidifying their commitment to God. We can be sure of the fact that this time, it was religion that drove the scheme more so than just greed. From that point forward, "none were admitted to join the company, only those of a truly moral character, either belonging to the church or abstaining from profane company." Roger, no longer strapped for time in running the séances, spent his nights visiting other churchgoers in the very same manner he visited the new conductor. The story was that the new Company would become the guardians of said treasure to allow the spirits to finally leave the world in peace and forever rest in Heaven. The treasure would then be revealed to them and left in their care. So Rogers became an overseer of a con, and the conductor in charge was too honest to realize he was part of a deception.

The new secret meetings occasionally saw Ransford partake in the prayers and such as if he were nothing but a mere Christian—a perfect cover for not being suspected of orchestrating the whole thing. During one of these transition meetings where Rogers was symbolically handing over conducting powers, the men first heard the spirit urging them to "Look to God!" After the ritual went about its usual routine, the men had gathered in a circle that then measured around thirty feet across to accommodate their new number of over twenty men. They held out their papers above their heads as they knelt with their faces to the ground with their eyes closed. This time, the message mentioned various chapters in the Bible that the members were compelled to read and particular Psalms they had to sing. It also mentioned the decree that all members had to "deposit into the hands of the spirit according to his circumstances, not exceeding twelve, nor less than six pounds, in order to relieve the spirit from his exigencies [requirements], that he might return from whence he came." The conductor finished the meeting by reading aloud the last part of the note, "O, faithful man! What more need I exhibit unto you! I am the spirit of a just man, sent from Heaven to declare these things unto you; and I can have no rest until I have delivered great possessions into your hands, but look to God, there is a greater treasure in Heaven for you! O, faithful me! Press forward in faith, and the prize is yours."

It was agreed that the money would be provided at the next meeting, where, after several ceremonies, prayers and rotations around a room, the men proceeded into a field about one hundred yards from Rogers's home. Once there, they again "drew a circle about twenty feet in diameter…[and] stepped within it, waiting for the spirit to make its appearance." Being the only one standing up, the conductor snapped to attention as a spirit appeared about sixty yards out amid smoke that seemed to come from nowhere— in actuality, it came from one of Ransford's chemical contraptions. Upon conversing with the spirit (one of Ransford's accomplices), the conductor, who was told to stay a safe distance from the spirit, instructed his men in possession of the money to exit the circle in order of their age (from youngest to oldest). They were then to place the money under a specified tree. Not all the men had the money or could afford what was asked of them; some brought only a couple of pounds, hoping the spirit might forgive their inadequacies. As they followed the conductor to the tree, the spirit appeared again. Speaking from about twenty yards out, it proclaimed, "Look to God!" The men were startled. Once the money was deposited under the tree, the men retreated to the circle in silent prayer. "They all returned to the house, observing the greatest order, trembling at every noise and gazing in every direction, supposing they were surrounded by hobgoblins, apparitions, witches and even the Devil himself." To further shed any suspicion, Ransford and one other conspirator also pretended to give up their money.

The collected loot of forty pounds was not as much as Rogers had expected but was still sufficient for the time being. Days later, the men were relieved to find out that they had successfully freed the spirit after Rogers visited the unsuspecting conductor once again in disguise. They also found out that the location of the protected treasure, which they were then made guardians of, would soon be revealed to them. But before that could take place, Ransford moved on to the second part of his plan. Naturally, there was no treasure to speak of that he could bring his constituents to, so instead, he changed the theme of his meetings. The impetus was then to degrade the Company's morals by raising feelings of guilt, unholiness and discrediting them in the eyes of their neighbors. With Rogers again placing himself at the head of his followers—supposedly at the spirit's wish—he told the men the ghost required them to consume spirits freely at the following meetings. This was directed as a means of celebration of the spirits' ascendance to Heaven. It was during this time, in 1789, that men "[who] before observed the greatest temperance" drank to the degree that often made them "incapable of navigating home." As initially intended by Rogers, the upright members of the towns from which they came were drawing a lot of negative attention. The normally well-respected citizens appeared to have lost all their morality, especially when appearing drunk in public. The Company's members attempted to straighten out their acts by attending church more frequently and refusing the hard cider pressed on to them at the meetings. It was also becoming more apparent to them that if they had confessed to speaking to and meeting with supernatural spirits that were forcing them to consume the otherworldly spirits, it would only further destroy their already shaky reputation. They were trapped—or simply, they were exactly where Ransford Rogers wanted them to be.

As Ransford handed each man in the Company a small sachet containing ground animal bones, he could not know that this would prove to be his final undoing. The parcels of burned and powdered bones were explained to have been the dust of the spirits' bodies, which he had received from them as a sign of their approbation.[18] Each man in the Company was told to guard the dust and keep it as a reminder of their great secret. While many did not want to take the parcel with them, it was again pressed on them to do so. It was the will of the spirits, Ransford proclaimed. This act sealed the men's obedience, as they would not want to be known to possess any such articles in their proper Christian homes. Subsequently, doing so would only make them more secretive about the whole endeavor. Rogers wanted to make sure that the people would not rise up against him and demand to see the treasure—at least until he found it appropriate for him to leave Morris County without bringing too much attention to himself. Blemishing their character within their communities and instilling the fear of God in them seemed like the perfect answer.

And then things fell apart. One of the aged members of the group, presumably one Alexander Carmichael, accidentally left his parcel of powder behind.[19] When his wife examined the contents of the small pouch— as her husband had yet again mysteriously ridden off into the night—Mrs. Carmichael was frightened. "What if it is witchcraft?" she worried. Being the good Christian woman she was, she carefully closed the sachet and took a horse from the stable after getting dressed. It was dark and had been quite a while since she had ridden, but she knew the reverend would surely know what to make of it. Perhaps it would not be too late to save her husband from eternal damnation.

It was late when her husband walked in the door. He was met by his wife of many years sitting at the kitchen table. Next to her was a short burning candle and, to his terror, a small parcel—the parcel. There was no point in trying to lie now; the secret was out. She insisted on knowing the contents of the package and the means by which he had acquired it. After some back and forth—and only when she reluctantly promised to keep his secret—the man divulged what had been occupying his time in the proceeding weeks and months. How could he have done such a thing, place so much shame on the family name? "[You are serving the Devil!]" she screamed. No, she would not keep this secret. It was her duty to put an end to this witchcraft. After all, even the reverend refused to touch the contents of the package in fear of it bewitching him in some way. The husband pleaded. She would ruin him, he said. Hoping his wife would see his reasoning in keeping the affair quiet so as not to ruin their family, the man left his home for the second time that night. When he arrived at Rogers's door, he could barely catch his breath. Ransford informed him that as long as he could keep his wife from telling the secret, all would be well. If he failed, the wrath of the spirits would befall them all.

3

THE CURTAIN FALLS

The moral of the story of Ransford Rogers and what is commonly known as the Morristown Ghost seems too obvious to be repeated. Still, while not everyone involved became wise enough to see through the veil of deception, at least one of the con man's disciples did. In fact, as Rogers scrambled to keep his con from falling apart in the weeks following Mrs. Carmichael's discovery, his anxiety was getting the best of him. As the elderly lady began to spread around town the secret news of witchcraft happening right in front of the unsuspecting citizens' noses, the people of Morristown and nearby towns began to look at Rogers suspiciously. He knew it, too. In a hastily convened meeting with his coconspirators, the master con man ordered his devotees to ramp up the ghost sightings to cement his followers' devotion further. In doing so, the men began to work around the clock, overexerting themselves beyond human capabilities. They all had to keep up the appearance of having authentic day jobs to not arouse any suspicions. Yet, night after night, the men set off, dressed in ghostly tattered clothing and armed with their voice-changing tools—presumably tin cans with hollowed-out holes through which they would speak—making communications with the members of their second con. Unfortunately for them, and specifically Ransford Rodgers himself, one could not go on too long and stay focused without proper rest. Add some lively alcohol to the equation, and the stage was set for the final act.

Ranford's meetings with his followers took on new fervor, as men began to share their stories of the spirits personally visiting them at their homes.

Rogers played this up as much as he could, telling everyone that the spirits were finally starting to trust everyone enough to appear to them directly. This was a good sign, he told them. The treasure would most definitely be revealed to them soon. On each occasion, the ghost's message was the same; everything would be all right "soon." One must not allow their faith to be shaken by gossipmongers and scandalmongers. Ransford just needed a few more days—perhaps weeks—to get enough money collected to make an adequate profit to settle his debts with his assistants and still come out on top. Only then could he, like the ghosts he invented, disappear forever. "Just a few more days," he thought. As recorded in the unauthored pamphlet that details the events that grace these pages, Rogers—with his anxiety getting the best of him—began to frequent local taverns in the early evening hours preceding his secret ghostly excursions. One particular evening, the con man had a little too much to drink. It was later reported that on that night, Ransford grabbed his chosen ghostly costume—supposedly, he favored the good old white, albeit dirty, sheet—and "rode out to a house of a certain gentleman in order to converse with him as a spirit." It would be his last appearance as the Morristown Ghost.

With the costume not quite fully covering his feet—a careless oversight surely attributed to his quasi-drunk state—Ransford could not hold the voice apparatus consistently close to his mouth. Something seemed a bit off to the man who was woken from his sleep by a tap on the window and then ordered

The Presbyterian church from which many members of the second "Company" were recruited. *Courtesy of the Morris County Historical Society.*

to come outside and stand by his gate. Of course, he was not to go an inch farther— he could not get too close to the "spirit." He did as he was told. Unknown to both of the men standing by the moonlight, one slurring his speech with his voice going in and out of its concealed state and the other intensively listening, the landowner's wife had slowly crept up to her bedroom window. She sat below the windowsill listening. Finally, she could not stand it anymore. Slowly, with her hands holding her up, she looked out. It was dark, yet not dark enough for her to miss the "spirit's" dirty shoes sticking out from the bottom of his disguise. She ducked back down. Did he see her? "After conversing with the man for some time and ultimately ending with a prayer, Rogers departed. But not before declaring himself the spirit of a just man." The farmer was ordered to go back inside and speak to nobody but other Company followers about his experience. To his surprise, when he entered his home, his eyes met his very distressed wife staring up at him from the floor by the window.

She did not let him sleep in the next morning, waking him up as soon as dusk was just starting to turn to dawn. It was foggy that morning. One had to strain their eyes to see anything more than a few yards ahead of them; yet that did not matter for the man. He was not there to look out onto the hidden horizon; all he needed to see was the ground a few feet in front of him. Putting on his heavy boots and a warm coat, the man stepped out of his home, and as he had discussed with his wife the night prior, he proceeded to carefully make his way to the area by the fence where the "spirit" had appeared just a few short hours earlier. As reported by the pamphlet's account, there had been heavy dew that night, which enabled the elderly gentleman to pick out what he was seeking without much difficulty. There in front of him, plain as day, were tracks of a man. Suddenly excited—perhaps even angry—the man called out for his wife to join him as they made their way around the house and stable, following the tracks to "the fence, where he perceived a horse had been tied." Not yet suspecting Rogers but then fully aware that he was indeed being duped, the man readied his horse and rode out carefully so as not to trample over the "other horse's" tracks. He followed them out of town. Before he even made it to his destination, he already knew what had happened. Somehow, he then felt as if he had always known. There was no such thing as ghosts, and there was no treasure, except the one he willingly gave away in the hopes of gaining more considerable riches. His horse came to a stop at the doorway of a house he knew all too well. Ransford Rogers was not home.

Following the tracks around the house, the angered man noticed more horse tracks leading away from home. He decided to continue his morning investigation. Rogers was found about a mile away, sleeping in the barn of a certain gentleman, who had loaned him the horse the evening prior. Scattered around him were a dirty sheet and what appeared to be a metal cup of sorts with punctured holes. As he stood there, looking at the con man, the gentleman decided to contact the proper authorities. He quickly but quietly hurried to rouse the owner of the barn and told him what had transpired. With one man keeping an eye on the still very much hungover and passed out Ransford, the other went into town to notify the proper authority. Within an hour, men descended on the barn, and after "consulting, and judging him culpable, [Rogers] was immediately apprehended and committed to prison." As he was led out of the barn with his hands bound by a rope, Ransford was not disoriented enough to not plead his case. This was a misunderstanding, he said. Someone was trying to discredit him.

According to the only known account of the events, the detection greatly alarmed the whole company, "as they were unwilling to believe that Rogers was the spirit, even when the clearest evidence demonstrated that he must have been the ghost in question." News of the great con man pretending to be a ghost spread like a wildfire. And although people began to suspect who the duped men were, nobody wanted to embarrass the otherwise respected churchgoing members of society—or even the members of the earlier con. Perhaps still hoping he could get out of this with his reputation somewhat preserved, Rogers, who continually professed his innocence, did not initially disclose the names of the members of the two Companies. With local authorities and the press hounding him to reveal the plot, the fallen con man also did not share the fact that he had accomplices, all of whom, by this time, had packed their bags and left Morris County, never to be seen or heard from again. Within a week, Rogers was bailed out by a gentleman "that I shall call by the name of Compassion," as stated the anonymous author of the first pamphlet. After being allowed to go home to await trial, Ransford was presumably assisted in his escape from the vicinity of Morristown by some of his followers who believed in the man's innocence to the very end. Yet his freedom was temporary, as he was once again apprehended after he was spotted riding out of town by another wife of one of his former supporters.

This time, upon his arrest, the defeated Ransford Rogers admitted to his crimes. He disclosed the specifics of his schemes and provided evidence for the capture of his accomplices, who were never caught. Similarly, he detailed the how, where and when of all his meetings with the first and second Companies. No one knows what would make him disclose all of this information, yet he did. And although the names of the people he swindled were not made public, it was soon obvious to those who cared enough to inquire which men had lost a total of $1,300 in 1700s currency, "none which was ever recovered by the unfortunate and humbugged company." While history does not record the means of Rogers's second escape, it nonetheless acknowledges that he once again eluded punishment. And although the man had escaped, all the damage was done. This time, none of the men he cheated seemed to stick by him, especially as the copious evidence of their ignorance was the talk of the town. Embarrassed, the men from both the first and the

The Old Morris County Courthouse on Morristown Green, where Ransford was tried. *Courtesy of the Morris County Historical Society.*

second con threatened to find Ransford and punish him accordingly. The author of the infamous pamphlet written a few short years after the event mocked the dichotomy, stating for posterity that "many threatening and horrid imprecations proceeded from many after this man, who only a few days before, they revered and thought [of as] a superior being." Luckily for all those involved, the pamphlet, the only surviving account of the story that many would go on to refer to as that of the Morristown Ghost, disputedly omitted any names of those involved—or did it? After all, not many have seen the pamphlet. Further shrouded in secrecy is the fact that the author chose to remain anonymous.

The main testament to the embarrassment of the men tricked by Ranford Rogers is plain for us to see today. The sheer fact that there are none but a few alleged surviving copies of the original pamphlet tells us that the men and their families did all they could to keep their naiveness from being recorded for posterity. In fact, when New York's W.W. Munsell and Co. published its *History of Morris County, New Jersey* in 1882, the editor acknowledged that the names of those involved would remain hidden, as there were many descendants of the affected prominent families still living in Morris County. Thus, we will perhaps never know whose ancestors allowed themselves to be led into a tale of the macabre and superstition—well, at least not all of them. The same cannot be said for Rogers, whose name is now synonymous with the events of 1788–90. We have the unnamed author of *The Morristown Ghost*, published in 1792, to thank for that. The author's belief was that this was a tale that needed to be told to rid the area, the state and the nation of the predisposed notions of evil spirits that they believed were hindering human progress. "But ought not the County of Morris to perpetuate and honor the name of Rogers for eradicating ignorance and causing the light of reason to illuminate the minds of many, where obscurity had reigned for many years?"

Attempting to distance their county from "the most vulgar and illiterate parts of the world, where the capricious notions of witchcraft and hobgoblins reside," the author decided to write the story, regardless of the implications it might have had on those involved.

> *It is not from malevolence, or any antipathy, against any person or place, that induced me to write the above-mentioned transactions, but purely to enlighten the minds of the simple and free them from the imaginary fear of witches, apparitions, and hobgoblins, which do not exist. And as this relation proceeds from one that wishes happiness to all mankind, and the author, although unknown, hopes that no one person or persons will be offended at the relation of facts, when there are no names mentioned; providing they had an active part with the anticipating fire-club. This pamphlet is chiefly intended for the perusal of the good economists in Morris County.*
> *Gentlemen, yours in amity,*
> *PHILANTHROPIST*

With these words, the amateur historian, narrator, journalist or just plain neighbor with a penchant for writing concluded their story of the Morristown Ghost. As for Ransford Rogers and his Company, their story was far from over. In fact, through historical detection and a deconstruction of events that transpired, it evolves into a new, more factual tale—a history.

PART II

THE ART OF HISTORICAL DETECTION

4

SCHOOLEY'S MOUNTAIN TREASURE

At the core of the events of 1788 was the legend of a Schooley's Mountain treasure. It was the probability of said treasure and the people's willingness to believe in its existence that formed the basis of Rogers's scam. So why did this treasure presumably exist in the first place? And why would it be buried at Schooley's Mountain? To answer those questions, we must turn to the civil war fought within the larger context of the American Revolution between 1770 and 1785. With Loyalists on one side and Patriots on the other, the Garden State—and Morris County—suffered terrible losses. Yet it was the vicious treatment of the county's Tories (Loyalists to the British Crown), the uncertainty of their futures and their continually revolving status that would make it more likely they would choose to hide their riches until a time when it was safe to retrieve them.

Moreover, reviewing the names of the known Loyalists from the area makes it evident that the social status they held in their respective communities might have correlated to a particular financial prowess. History did not record the origins of the assumption of gold and silver being buried in a remote area on Schooley's Mountain, yet we know that the belief in its existence was genuine in the years following the exodus of the area's Tories. The locals, whether from the desperation of seeing their lands ravished by war, prewar jealousy or simple greed, desperately wanted to believe in a treasure that just might have been buried in their backyard. Thus, while it is highly unlikely that a treasure ever existed, the likelihood of certain Morris County gentlemen believing otherwise is very real.

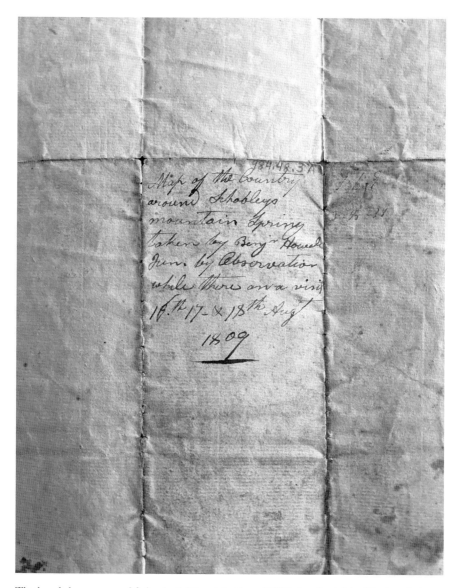

The hand-drawn map of Schooley's Mountain from 1809 is barely visible. The inscription on the back reads: "Map of the country around Schooley's Mountain Spring taken by Beny [*sic*]…by observation while there." *Courtesy of the Morris County Historical Society.*

The end of the war in 1783, just five years before Ransford's con, had finally allowed the people of New Jersey to take stock of the terrible losses they and their state had suffered. Speaking of the war, Reverend Colin of Swedesboro, New Jersey, recalled "everywhere distrust, fear, hatred and abominable selfishness.…Parents and children, brothers and sisters, wife and husband, were enemies to one another…[with men] plundering and destroying everything in a barbarous manner, cattle, furniture, clothing, and food…whipping and imprisoning each other."[20] Apart from the psychological and physical damage to the state's inhabitants, the Revolutionary War had destroyed the entire landscape of New Jersey. Hardly a church or a school building in any of the towns had been left untouched. Wherever the armies marched or irregulars and militias raided, they had left scars on the landscape. In Middlesex County, one of the three counties with the highest population of accused Tories, 655 properties belonging to various individuals were damaged.[21] The state was a battlefield as much to the grand armies of the British and Patriots as it was to the citizens who fought a greater yet underrated battle for their place within their local communities. Looking at the state of affairs, one would be hard-pressed to denounce the Loyalists' desire to protect their personal property, even if keeping their land was nearly impossible.

Dennis P. Ryan, an assistant editor of *The Papers of William Livingston* and a speaker at the "Revolution in East Jersey," an annual New Jersey history symposium, in 1972, had examined Loyalist enlistment in the most famous Tory militia unit in the state; namely, Cortland Skinner's Loyalist New Jersey Volunteers. He concluded that more than one-third, or over 50,000, of the state's inhabitants were Loyalists. According to his findings, out of the six battalions created in 1776 and disbanded in 1783, 2,450 men actively served in its ranks. While this figure seems small when placed in the context of the entire state population, Ryan concluded that many did not join the official British forces outright due to fear of repercussion. In turn, they showed their displeasure by joining irregular bands and/or raiding parties that targeted their Patriot neighbors.[22] Yet once all the wives and children of those who joined Skinner's Volunteers were accounted for—as well as vague numbers of those who served in the unofficial raiding bands—he concluded that apart from the Patriots and the uninterested Quakers, the Loyalists accounted for anywhere between one-third to one-half of the state's population. In fact, during the halfway point of the conflict, there were more New Jerseyans serving in the British ranks than there were serving George Washington in New Jersey's

Continental brigades. As for Morris County, where the events surrounding the Morristown Ghost took place, Richard T. Irwin's detailed study of the area uncovers nearly 80 confirmed Loyalist families. Many were identified through land confiscation records compiled at the end of the war.[23]

While not all Loyalists in Morris County were easily identified and many were never "found out" by their neighbors, the ones who were uncovered often belonged to the wealthier landowning class of the area. Generally speaking, they had also accumulated a certain social status and hence a wealth that came with it. Some of the more recognizable Morris County Loyalists of the time were Anglican minister Peter Kemble of Morris Township; deputy land surveyor general for New Jersey Thomas Millidge and his son, Stephen Millidge; two wealthy landowners, Ezekiel Beach and Philip Van Cortlandt; two business owners, Thomas White and Thomas Welcher; and the Hutchinson and Bowlsby families, who had numerous family members tried for treason.[24] Searching through local newspapers from the last years of the Revolutionary War, one comes across an advertisement that names all of the men previously mentioned as "having taken an active part with the enemy, [and being] expatriated and their estates confiscated." The advertisement granted Commissioners Alexander Carmichael (the same man who would come to be swindled by Ransford Rogers and whose wife discovered the parcel of dust) and Aaron Kitchell (more about his role in the Morristown Ghost con later) the right to offer for sale "the houses, lands and leases for life and all the real estate that belongs to [the men listed previously]."[25] These were just a few of the names of the area's Tories—ones that best showcase the possible collective wealth that might have been hidden on Schooley's Mountain. All the men highlighted were known to possess a certain amount of wealth. Having said that, there were nearly one hundred families in Morris County who were labeled as Loyalists, and thus, while they may not have had as much money as the families previously listed, they still would have been inclined to hide and protect their valued possessions. Those wealthy community members who were not executed for treason—as was the case with many of the Hutchinson family members—had their lands and property confiscated throughout the war, and many moved out of the area.

As to whether any of the assumed wealth was left over for the Loyalists of Morris County to hide after the bitter civil struggle that ensued, that is another story. What we do know is that it was a common opinion at the time that the men of this wealthy class hid their money in Schooley's Mountain, a range of highlands about twenty miles outside of Morristown proper. It was best described as a wild and desolate place. The level plateau, some 1,200 feet above the sea level, was one of the highest points in the entire state of New Jersey.[26] There was also one mystical component to said mountain range. It was believed at the time and many years after that the Lenape Natives occupied Schooley's Mountain for its springs and waters, which drew healing powers from the iron deposits found in the nearby mountains.[27] The allure was so strong that the mountain become one of the nation's first summer resorts by 1815, drawing people to its waters, which promised to heal a plethora of disorders. Still, there is no real significance of the place and why it would be chosen to hold a buried treasure apart from its remote and mysterious location. Together with its elevation, it was that much more difficult to access, at least by those too lazy to make the trek. And this is all considering that said treasure even existed. The war between the Patriots and Loyalists was vicious enough that the supporters of the Crown might not have had any money left to hide. And while both sides caused unspeakable carnage, it was the Loyalists who ultimately paid the highest price. Like a revolving door, the actions of each side were dependent on which army was occupying the state and the county at that given time. As the British mostly lost control of the area by the late 1770s, it was the Patriots who ultimately triumphed.

Postcard from late 1800s showing the Spring House Resort grounds on Schooley's Mountain. *Courtesy of the Morris County Historical Society.*

Schooley's Mountain Academy.

THIS institution is now in successful operation & recommends itself to the patronage of an enlightened public.

The advantages possessed by this site for a literary institution are probably not exceeded by any in the state.

The branches taught in it are such as are intended to prepare for College or business, viz: Latin and Greek languages, Mathematics, Mechanics, English Grammar and language, Geography, &c.

The terms are *one hundred dollars* per annum, including, board, tuition washing and every necessary except books. The tuition fee, twelve dollars and fifty cents semi-annually to be paid in advance.

The winter session commences the last day of October and will continue till the 1st of April, when there will be a public examination and rewards of approbation bestowed on deserving pupils.

As there is a prospect of a considerable accession, it is desirable that those, who may wish to enter their children into this school, should make seasonable application. Address to E. Marsh, Esq. or,

Rev. H. WHITFIELD HUNT, A. M.
Principal.
Schooley's Mountain, Oct. 4, 1826, 93*4

A newspaper advertisement for Schooley's Mountain Academy from 1826. *From the* Sussex Register, *Newton, NJ.*

With Washington's armies retreating through the state in 1775, the Loyalists moved across New Jersey in small groups, burning, robbing and, in some instances, murdering Patriots. The mere appearance of British troops in a locality sparked fierce action against Patriot neighbors, with Patriot farmers often spending most nights hiding out in the woods and returning at daybreak to work their fields.[28] Similarly, as soon as the British left, the Patriots came out, and the Loyalists were beaten and dragged off. And as was often the case in the latter part of the war, the Loyalists' property was confiscated by the state.[29] While the negative aspects of the Loyalists made for a perfect good guy versus bad guy narrative, the Patriots' actions were equally vicious. By 1776, some counties had resorted to sending Patriot raiding parties throughout the state, burning specific houses and capturing Loyalists. Such savagery toward British sympathizers was justified in the minds of New Jerseyans due to the reckless cruelty of the British Loyalists who themselves often attacked without warning, set fire to homes and churches and, most importantly, acted out of premeditation (often settling old scores from prewar times).[30]

During this game of cat and mouse between American general Washington's and British general Howe's forces between 1775 and 1777, as the armies marched and retreated through New Jersey, the state became engulfed in spoil, chaos and destruction. These events might explain why, after the war, the people of the area thought of themselves as deserving of Loyalist riches that were seemingly hidden during the later stages of the conflict. To them, they had earned the treasure through what they had endured at the hands of Loyalists during the bloody conflict. With the proximity of the British army, the Tories who had remained in hiding up to that point came out in great numbers. General Howe's offer of a full pardon and protection of property to all who would denounce the Rebels' cause was at once answered by over two thousand families. Loyalist farmers, rejoicing at seeing the king's troops, hurried to them with offers of assistance, placed their wagons at their disposal for the transportation of stores and went about gathering provisions.[31] More importantly, however, a number of houses and gristmills belonging to once outspoken Patriots were burned down. The pro-Americans, being natural targets of Tory revenge, were pointed out to the British forces, with the houses of local militiamen and those who were members of the new Revolutionary government specifically targeted. Estates became forfeited, seized and destroyed; even goods that had been left in the safekeeping of friends by fugitive Patriots could not escape the prying eyes of those who worked with tireless and uncanny efficiency and hatred.[32] "Stop the Robbers! ONE HUNDRED DOLLARS REWARD," cried an advertisement in the *Pennsylvania Evening Post* on December 28, 1776. "Last Tuesday, three villains came to the house of Mr. Nowel Furman, near Princeton, and after abusing the family in a barbarous manner, took with them goods to the amount of between one and two hundred pounds....Whoever secures said goods and the men so that they be convicted shall have ONE HUNDRED DOLLARS!"[33]

Robbery and pillaging were nevertheless not the furthest extent of damage done to the state's Patriots. The more pressing issue became the acts of violence directed against individuals. The *New York Gazette* reported in early January 1777 the death of one Isaac Pearson Esq., who "endeavoring to pass through the Jerseys...was last week murdered by some of the rebellious Banditti who infest the public roads between this city and Philadelphia."[34] Until the news of Princeton's and Washington's victory over General Lord Cornwallis began to be openly discussed in local newspapers, Loyalist vigilantes remained active throughout the state. Midnight terrorism became a part of every Patriot family in New Jersey; farms were set ablaze, and all of their valuable goods were stolen. Likewise, Patriot leaders and their known friends were murdered and/or kidnapped to be sent to British prisons in New York.[35] Anticipating the massive retaliation at the hands of local Patriots, General Washington attempted to preserve order and not let the situation in New Jersey get out of hand. Needing the people of the state to concentrate on assisting his forces, coupled with the fear of provoking an inner conflict that would detract them from the larger war, the general announced in the *Pennsylvania Evening Post* on January 1, 1777, that he "strictly forbids all of the officers and soldiers of the Continental army of the militia and all recruiting parties, plundering any person whatsoever, whether Tories or others. The effects of such persons will be applied to public uses in a regular manner, and it is expected that humanity and tenderness to women and children will distinguish brave Americans, contending for liberty, from mercenary ravages."

As a result of the Battle of Princeton, General Cornwallis chose to move most of the British troops out of the state of New Jersey. What remained was a newly reinvigorated spirit of the local Patriots, who then saw the military situation shift in their favor. As a result of his army's brave actions, Washington's proclamation was ignored.

The rise of anger and bitterness against the guerrilla activities of the local Tories through the majority of the month of December (1776) and early January (1777) had infused the Patriots' determination to retaliate with equal savagery. The events that transpired during this time also become significant to the investigation of the legend of the Schooley's Mountain Treasure and the possibility or likelihood of such a treasure existing. As historian Leonard Lundin pointed out, when Howe's forces were spread out throughout the state in the winter of 1776, the Americans had paid for their harshness to the Tories during the preceding months; now that the British troops had been driven away, the revolutionaries avenged themselves upon their political opponents for what they had suffered at the hands of the British military and local guerrilla attacks.[36] The vengeance that followed throughout the few months after Howe and Cornwallis had retreated back to New York for the winter in January 1777 was heartless and cruel. The situation had turned around so much so that the *Pennsylvania Evening Post*'s January 30 edition proclaimed, "We are informed, from good authority, that many of the inhabitants…in New Jersey, who received written protections [from the British troops], are now determined to return them to His Britannic Majesty's commissioners."[37] The failure of the British to remain in the state for the rest of the conflict had sealed the Loyalists' fate. Chiefly, with the British retreating, the many Tories who had openly come out in their support of the British during the first couple months of the war were then left to fend for themselves.

By the end of January, the *New York Gazette* and *Weekly Mercury* were reporting occurrences of Patriot—or as the pro-British newspapers called it, Rebel—activity. Opening the article was a description of numerous stores and houses being pillaged and goods exceeding a value of £1,000 being carried away from a certain Loyalist family. The article summed up the situation in New Jersey: "Daily accounts are received of their ravages in the back country, where they fancy themselves out of reach, upon the poor miserable inhabitants, who either do not countenance or concur in their proceedings." It concluded:

Dr. Leddell's mills, which were heavily used by the Continental army during its time in Morris County. *Courtesy of the Morris County Historical Society.*

The home of Dr. Leddell. *Courtesy of the Morris County Historical Society.*

And such is the system of liberty established in those colonies, not under the influence of His Majesty's arms, that no man dares to express his opinion relative to this mob-government, without incurring the forfeiture of all his property, and the confinement of his person in a prison.... Thus whole families, once in affluence, are reduced to wretchedness and beggary without even the usual consolation of the common pity; for such is the brutal fury of these Rebels, that no extremity of vengeance is thought severe enough for those, whom they know or suspect to have any attachment to the king and constitution.[38]

Throughout the month of January, New York newspapers reported various accounts of theft, plunder, family abuse and even cases of rape at the hands of the New Jersey militia and individual citizens of the state. Those Loyalists who could flee to nearby New York did; those who could not were never again able to proclaim their allegiance to the Crown as they had done only a few months prior.

The newly appointed governor of New Jersey William Livingston organized a Council of Safety, which sought out, tried and punished all those suspected of disloyalty to the American cause. The organization soon began to offer Loyalists a choice between death and enlistment. In Morristown—of the later Morristown Ghost fame—the local court had sentenced thirty-five Tories to be hanged; after two had died, the rest promptly volunteered for the regular state militia. Similarly, in 1779, the same was true for all but two out of more than seventy Loyalists who were offered the same choice.[39] Meanwhile, the mistreatment of Tories throughout the state and Morris County continued. In a letter to a friend, dated July 5, 1777, an unnamed Morristown citizen proclaimed, "[American Patriots] burnt, stripped and destroyed all as they went along....[Many] women and children were left without food to eat....They even destroyed books they came across; this I assert as a fact."[40]

By the last year of the war, 1783, the situation in New Jersey had become so bad that its governor William Livingston was forced to address the issue publicly. Condemning the practice of looting, the governor asserted that the action, "however it attempted to be vindicated under pretense of inflicting condign punishment on the internal enemies of our country, is not only repugnant to the laws of the land...but hath a manifest tendency to inflame the minds of the sufferers; to excite jealousies and contentions between the inhabitants, at the time when we ought to be peculiarly studious of cultivating unanimity and concord."[41] The proclamation called for stricter

Morristown's Jacob Ford Mansion. It was one of the first house museums in the nation and the home of the most famous member of the Ford family. This house served as George Washington's headquarters during the Revolutionary War. *Photograph by the author.*

rules of the local militias in allowing soldiers to go on their own without proper supervision and also called for the officers to keep their eyes open for any unlawful activities on the part of the local citizens throughout the state. Yet while the governor spoke of the discriminatory behavior toward the many Tories as an act that was illegal, considering the state's laws, he knew that he was powerless to actually enforce any law prohibiting it. In fact, it would not be a stretch to assert that the governor's proclamation was just an act of appeasement aimed at General Washington, who was very much disturbed by the situation around him. He witnessed it while he and his armies were stationed in Morristown, New Jersey, on two separate occasions.

The events that transpired in the Garden State during the war are important to keep in mind when assessing the probability of a hidden Tory treasure. The motive was certainly there for those who had any worthy possessions to hide. While it becomes more likely that such treasure could have been hidden when looking at the situation closely, the same cannot be said for the assumption that the loot even existed in the first place. Those who were considered Tories in Morris County were hunted down and stripped of all their possessions long before they could bind together to hide them collectively. As the evidence shows, most if not all were left impoverished and landless and were often chased out of the area by the war's end. Furthermore, always under their neighbors' scrutiny, those who remained loyal to the Crown throughout the conflict were always in the minority and were never allowed to congregate in groups—nor would they want to, as drawing attention to themselves would, sure enough, bring about further persecution. By the end of the war, the Morris County Tories were all but gone, and those who remained were reduced to a poor man's status.

With the lawful confiscation of Loyalists' land, cattle and horses, one would be hard-pressed to believe that such men would not try to reclaim their alleged wealth after the war's end. Nevertheless, there is no record of any of the area's Tories coming into any wealth following the conflict. According to the 1792 pamphlet detailing the events of the Morristown Ghost, there were "several persons murdered and buried with the money [at Schooley's Mountain, or Schooler Mountain, as it was known as at the time]." It was the spirits of those buried with the treasure that were believed to have been guarding it. This assertion is also highly unlikely, as many people at the time were in dire need of money due to the strains of war, and Tory property was always the go-to bounty. It would make no sense to bury the "gold and silver" for a later date. The disruption caused by local pillaging and warfare caused a dire strain on the locals. There were many documented occurrences in which both Tory and Patriot citizens awoke in the morning to see their barns broken into and animals taken. One needs to look no further than General Washington's proclamation in the *New Jersey Gazette* on January 21, 1778: "I hereby enjoin and require all persons, residing within seventy miles of my headquarters [in Morristown] to thresh one-half of their grain by the fifth day of February, and the other half by the fifth day of March… in case of failure of having all that shall remain in sheaves after the period above-mentioned, seized by the commissaries and quarter masters of the army."[42] The people of Morris County did not have the luxury or the time to bury any treasure to save for a time of need. For them, the time of need was taking place then and there.

Still, some locals remembered the Loyalists' riches of years prior to the war, and with feelings of hatred and bitterness left over from the war years, they were blinded to the fact that said families' wealth had been taken away from them long before 1788, or even 1783 for that matter. It goes without

Schooley's Mountain Seminary rendering from the mid-1800s. *Courtesy of the Morris County Historical Society.*

saying that within five years of the conflict, there were still many who sought the hypothetical treasure. With the Schooley's Mountain location predetermined as the supposed hiding place, many looked, but none found what was claimed to have been buried there. With strong beliefs in the treasure's existence and the cumbersome inability to locate it, the seekers were out of ideas and justifications for their failure to do so. There had to be a reason they could not find it. And as this was the 1780s, there could only have been one logical—or by today's standards, quite illogical—explanation. The treasure was hidden and guarded by supernatural spirits.

BELIEFS AND SUPERSTITIONS

T he belief in magic, witchcraft and astrology arrived in the American colonies through the plethora of European settlers who brought such views with them across the Atlantic. In Europe and the colonies, witchcraft was punishable by death. In fact, it is estimated that between the years 1400 and 1800, over fifty thousand people were executed in Europe after being convicted of witchcraft.[43] Once brought over to the Americas, the belief in the supernatural quickly found an existence alongside the more mainstream religious dogmas. By the late 1600s, there were about 150 separate witchcraft trials throughout the colonies; they were mostly small and insignificant compared to the infamous Salem Witch Trials of 1692.[44] And while the verdict of acquittal was the most common conclusion to these trials, the sheer number of people who were accused and the reasons for their suspicion convey a specific picture of the beliefs that many people held at the time. Early settlers, specifically those in the New England colonies, believed in supernatural interventions in the world's affairs, with evil sources having a hand in affecting daily life.[45] These included lightning striking one house instead of another, which was seen as an act of God, or epidemics targeting Natives instead of white settlers. Similarly, when something was logically hard to explain—like a child being stillborn or certain crops failing—it was often blamed on witchcraft or the Devil himself.

As stated in *The History of Morris County, New Jersey*, "It is not remarkable that people of a century ago should have believed in witches and hobgoblins....

The said people of this [Morris County] vicinity were no exception to the general belief of that time in ghosts."[46] The unauthored pamphlet of 1792—which was possibly written by the criminal Ransford Rogers himself—added, "It is obvious to all who are acquainted with the County of Morris that the phenomena and capricious notions of witchcraft, has engaged the attention of many of its inhabitants for a number of years, and the existence of witches is adopted by the generality of the people."[47] As the eighteenth century progressed, less educated folks still believed in witchcraft and the supernatural. Still—and truth be told—many of the people residing in rural areas of the nation, as was the case in Morris County, New Jersey, could not be considered highly educated. According to New Jersey historian John T. Cunningham, education in the area was limited, and illiteracy was still common. Most girls and boys, if they went to school at all, learned only basic reading and writing. Few girls continued school beyond the age of six—except among Quakers—but some boys received enough schooling to conduct business or church affairs. It was believed that girls needed only enough math skills to count eggs, skeins of wool, yards of cloth or the stitches they wove.[48]

Coupled with a simple agricultural lifestyle and the fear of the unknown and/or unexplainable, this low level of education made the day-to-day existence in colonial Morris County quite difficult. It was a backcountry, one with an older way of life that was losing ground to the new, more cosmopolitan, urban and education-based modern lifestyle. Tools were scarce, and everything had to be saved, as stores were rare and cash was almost nonexistent. Every nail, board, candle, piece of soap, article of clothing and nearly everything else was handmade.[49] Death and uncertainty were always near. Women often died in childbirth, and many children also died within a few short hours or days of being born. Smallpox, measles, pneumonia, influenza and blood poisoning took many people's lives. "Medical knowledge [in the backcountry of Morris County] was closer to witch doctor days than to science," wrote Cunningham.[50] In fact, when one takes a walk through any old cemetery in Morris County and looks at the grave markers, one will quickly notice the abundance of markers for infants, children dead before the age of ten and "young mothers who died in childbirth or young fathers felled by overwork, disease or the ignorance of doctors."[51] Such was the atmosphere in colonial New Jersey leading up to, throughout and shortly after the American Revolutionary War. In a sense, it was a climate ripe for frustrations toward unexplained afflictions and, above all, distrust.

The Old Tuttle House on Jockey Hollow Road. *Courtesy of the Morris County Historical Society.*

The most detailed account of the lifestyle of colonials and their predisposition to believing in the supernatural comes from the primary research gathered by Reverend Joseph F. Tuttle, DD, the president of Wabash University in Indiana and one of the first official historians of Morris County. Through various essays and contributions to the New Jersey Historical Society beginning in the mid- to late 1800s, the amateur historian detailed the fruits of his labor, namely the countless interviews he conducted with those who were still alive who had lived in the vicinity of Morris County at the time and recalled Ransford Rogers's con. Writing for the *Historical Magazine* in 1872, he stated: "Who has not heard of 'The Morristown Ghost?' Eighty-four years ago—1788—this famous character excited more notice in New Jersey than the putting of the new Constitution in motion. [The United States Constitution was published that very same year]."[52] Tuttle admits that he did get a chance to gaze upon one—perhaps the only surviving—copy of the original pamphlet. He did this courtesy of a Newark antiquary, Samuel H. Conger Esq. Since his mention of doing so in the 1800s, the pamphlet has not been located or seen since.

In his essay, the reverend wrote, "Some, very recently, were living who remembered the scenes; and a few years ago, the number of these was quite large….From them, I have learned many curious facts which have never been published." In reference to the general condition of society at the time, he quoted a letter written by a then recently deceased Reverend Peter Kanouse, who was old enough to give testimony as an eyewitness to the events. He referred to the Morris County region in question as "Rockaway Valley."

We have rambled over this ancient field as far back as I dare venture, when witches and hobgoblins held their powwows in the Old Indian burying ground, just as you go down to the Beaver Brook on the east side as you approach Dixon's dwelling in Rockaway Valley. And when the witches burnt down Old Charlotteburg Iron Works, I heard a lady say they metamorphosed her aunt into a horse and, after riding her to the place of rendezvous, tied her to a tree, where she witnessed the bonfire and their devil

*dance! Will-o-the-wisp was a spook often seen by the timid ones along the
Rockaway River from the Owl-kill up to Dover and farther, too. My early
schoolmates and myself had many a frightful race past the graves of old
Yommer and Pero, two Africans who knew all the arts of fetichism. Then,
elf-shooting was often witnessed—for instance, a sow shot though from
side to side, with a ball of hair, without wounding the skin! It was an
age of necromancy and heathenish superstition, when men were prepared
to be duped by such impostors as "the Morristown Ghost." Witchcraft
and fortune-telling were in vogue...and some obscure, yet honest, ignorant,
kind-hearted matron, bowed with age and face furrowed over with years,
was regarded with terror, and her oracles esteemed as if uttered by a very
Pythoness! Spooks and Will-o-the-wisps were often seen and were frequently
made the sober theme of the domestic circle when seated before the good old-
fashioned fire on a cold wintry night. There were some astrologers and now
and then one who used divination and could detect rogues and thieves and
find stolen property. The wonderful old almanac, with the waterman or
water-bearer, surrounded by the twelve signs, was full of curious cuts and
was often read more than the Bible.*[53]

Tuttle's research also pointed to the general widespread ignorance in the
area. Accordingly, schools were very few in number in Morris County and
were "taught by strolling itinerants who were not of a kind to correct the
popular superstitions of the times."[54] The historian added that most of the
teachers in Morris County came from New England and Ireland, and "facts
are still remembered [at the time of the research in 1850s], which show that
many of them were either superstitious or artful, since they did [so] little to
fasten the yoke of bondage on all within their reach."

The reverend also spoke of one Jacob Losey, who, before his death,
informed him that long after the Morristown Ghost was exposed, one of the
principal actors in that affair was building a dam for the Dover Iron Works.
While doing so, the man had "mystic horseshoes" nailed up in such positions
as not merely to keep the witches from entering the workers' bodies but to
also keep them from distracting or disturbing the men's work.[55] The man,
who lived near Morristown, would supposedly rather live without a roof
over his head and/or a fireplace to warm him up on the coldest days than
not have his home readied against mischievous spirits.

As for others who were alive in 1788, when Rogers evoked the
Morristown Ghost, they could still remember the widespread news of the
witch trials of Burlington County, New Jersey, from 50 years prior. On

October 22, 1730, readers of the *Pennsylvania Gazette* stared at a front-page story detailing the "With Trial of Mount Holly." Allegedly written as a satire by none other than Benjamin Franklin, the account has been printed and reprinted for more than 250 years since. Today, some call it a hoax, while others steadfastly defend its credibility. Still, whether real or not, the story did appear in the famed paper, and if nothing else, it sheds further light on the outdated and sometimes eccentric beliefs of the people of this area. State historian Frank R. Stockton asserted that nearly all the older towns in New Jersey had their ghost stores, witch stories and traditions of hidden treasures that were guarded by the ghosts of people who had been killed and buried with them. These spirits or charms would frighten away anyone trying to find said treasure.

> In Burlington, were two great trees which were regarded with admiration and fear by many of the inhabitants. One was a large willow tree, which was called the Witches' Tree, around which these horrible spirits were supposed to dance on many a wild night. Another was the Pirates' Tree, a great walnut, under the roots of which many of the inhabitants firmly believed that the famous Blackbeard and his band had buried many pots of gold, silver, and precious stones; and there these pots would have been dug up had it not been for the dear that the spirit of the savage pirate, who had been buried with the treasure, would have been the first thing to meet the eyes of the sacrilegious disturber of the pirate treasure vault.[56]

Stockton acknowledged that there were many more ghost stories of other places in New Jersey from around the time, but Morristown would eventually take the lead with having the most infamous one in the case of the Morristown Ghost.

Prior to the Ransford séances, it was the Mount Holly Witch Trial that got the most publicity. On the evening of October 12, 1730, in a small New Jersey town, there were over three hundred people who turned out to witness the case against a man and a woman accused of witchcraft. The charge: "making their neighbors' sheep dance in an uncommon manner and with causing hogs to speak, and sing Psalms, &c. to the great terror and amazement of the king's good and peaceable subjects in this providence."[57] The townspeople decided that the two had to go through witch trials to test their innocence. However, there was a twist to the story, as the accused couple called out their accusers—also a married couple—to prove their purity along with them. Upon their agreement and after a blessing by a local magistrate, both couples began their trials. As it was common knowledge that a Bible would always outweigh a witch, a test of scales opened the proceedings. Many shouts were coming from the crowd as "the wizard was first put in the scale and over him was read a chapter out of the Books of Moses, and then the Bible was put in the other scale (which was up to that point being held down)." Everyone gasped when as soon as the scale was let go with only the Bible on it, on the other side, "flesh and bones came down plump, and outweighed the [Bible] by abundance." The mob of people was not satisfied, as the experiment yielded the same result for the remaining four people participating. Screams of "Trial by water!" erupted.[58]

As the mob began moving toward the millpond, all grew eerily solemn. Hundreds watched both the accused and the accusers be stripped, with the women allowed to keep their bloomers on as to maintain a sense of decency. The trial by water—or witch dunking, as it was known at the time—determined one's guilt by a means of floating, as witches were known to reject the waters of baptism and would not sink. The two couples were individually bound by the hand and foot and loaded onto boats. Once out to the desired depth, the bodies were "placed in water, lengthways, from the side of a barge, having for security only a rope about the middle of each, [which was] held by someone in the [boat]." To the gasps of many who managed to get a front seat at the shore, all but the man doing the accusing floated as if by supernatural means. "A sailor in the [boat] jumped out upon the back of the accused Witch man, thinking to drive him down to the bottom, but the person bound, without any help, came up some time before the other." But then there was the curious case of the accusing woman, who, like her accused witch counterpart, also did not sink.

Not wanting to condemn a presumably innocent woman, the magistrate and the town council decided that the test needed to be repeated. When her body remained above water yet again, the panicked woman proclaimed that "she believed that the accused had bewitched her to make her so light and that she would be dunked again a hundred times, but she would dunk the Devil out of her." The more the people thought about it, and with much conferring with some in the crowd, it was determined that the test was not reliable because the woman's undergarments were helping her stay afloat. As such, the test would have to be repeated later for all involved, when they could be "properly" naked and without hundreds of people gawking at them. It was also decided that such a test should be postponed until the summer next, when the weather and water temperature would be more accommodating. The story ended without a verdict, and its follow-up never appeared in the *Pennsylvania Gazette* or any other publication. The intent here is not to determine the validity of the story but to use the significance of its publication at the given time and place. The citizens of New Jersey during the eighteenth century still very much believed in fables and the supernatural, even when new scientific explanations debunked them. This, of course, could be attributed to the fact that the small villages across the state were not necessarily privy to scientific education.

According to the *Morristown Ghost Fac-Simile* pamphlet, the area around Morristown was still riddled with cases of witchcraft in 1780s. "I was once in Morristown and happened to be in conversation with some gentlemen who had, as it were, the faith of assurance in witchcraft," wrote the anonymous author in 1792. "They informed me that there were several young women who were bewitched; and they had been harassed so much by witches for a long time, and all their experiments proved abortive, and the young women were so much debilitated they were fearful they would never recover their health."[59] It was the opinion of the author that such beliefs and opinions of locals made them "predisposed for…the reception of marvelous curiosities," as was the case during the 1788 Morristown Ghost incident.[60] These events were corroborated by historian John L. Brooke in his study of Mormon cosmology. In his research, he quoted another account of women in Morris County being "harassed by witches" and being "apprehensive of witches riding them."[61] While the anonymous pamphleteer was told of various supposed occurrences of witchcraft in the vicinity of Morris County, he admittedly thought them too trivial to repeat. Still, he did mention some curiosities that further supported his assertion that believing in witchcraft, ghosts and hobgoblins was not out the norm for the locals who would soon be introduced to the spirits guarding the Schooley's Mountain treasure.

There was the curious case of an old lady that was brought up by the author of the original pamphlet, in which she concluded, after churning butter for days without any success of obtaining a result, that "witches were in the churn." Fatigued, the woman went about seeking a remedy, and after some counsel, she arrived at heating several horseshoes and then placing them alternatively in the churn in hopes of "burning the devil out of it." It was reported that she immediately obtained butter. Reverend Joseph F. Tuttle, DD, was also able to obtain another similar account from the period, which he had "from the lips of a very intelligent man," who described what he saw:

> *When a young man, he was, one cold day at the house of a deacon* [whose name was withheld by Tuttle], *in the vicinity of Morristown. The*

deacon's wife was churning; but the butter would not come. "The witches are busy," said the good man; "bring me the iron wedge!" He put that useful instrument into the fire, and having heated it thoroughly, he told him to take off the churn lid, and he would fix the witches. In went the hot wedge, causing the refractory cream to boil and bubble furiously. "That will bring her out," said the old man complacently. Hardly had this ceremony been finished when his own niece, a girl of sixteen, came in; and the deacon addressed her in a very stern manner; "I thought I would bring you out, quick! You have taken up the trade early; but I will follow you till you have got enough of it! I guess you have got the mark of the hot wedge on you. I warrant you have!" The poor girl was greatly frightened; and her aunt took her out of the sight of her indignant kinsman. As soon as she left the room, the deacon said to my informant; "The wedge did the thing to for her; and if you could only examine, you would find where it burnt her!"[62]

In yet another occurrence, the anonymous Morristown Ghost pamphleteer outlined the case of a Morristown man who drove his sheep from his grain. Noticing one of the sheep had broken its leg while jumping over a fence, the man killed it immediately so as not to spread its bewitchment to the rest of the flock. Around the same time, an old lady, thrown off her horse on her way back from church was labeled as a witch by the community, who saw it as a sign that God no longer wanted her to attend mass. "And in fact, if a horse had a bellyache," proclaimed the 1792 pamphlet, "or any beast was in agony of pain and behaved uncommon, the general opinion was that the creature was bewitched."

While today, many would not admit to believing in witches and ghosts, the origins of such reluctance in fact goes back to the late eighteenth century, when science and reason prevailed. After the infamous Salem Witch Trials of the late 1600s, many colonies (and eventually states) reduced their punishments for the crimes of witchcraft. Some went as far as abolishing any and all such laws that might have given credibility to what was quickly becoming mythical. Records indicate that the last official witchcraft trial in the mainland colonies took place in Virginia in 1730; five years later, Parliament repealed the Witchcraft Act of 1604, the statue under which British American colonists prosecuted accused witches.[63] Still, the year 1788 was not that far removed, and those who were alive at the time were not quick to forget their ancestors' superstitions. According to the *New Jersey American History and Genealogy Project*, unlike the New England persecutions and killings of accused witches, New Jerseyans took them a bit less seriously—it was more of a curiosity than a crime. Still, as written in the 1960s by Frank R. Stockton, one of the state's more well-known historians, enough people believed in old superstitions "that it was often unsafe, or at least unpleasant, to be an ugly old woman or a young woman in not very good health, for it was believed that into such bodies the evil spirits delighted to enter."[64]

There is no record of anybody being burned at the stake in New Jersey or having suffered death because of witchcraft. In fact, there was no fanaticism present among the diverse population of the state as there was in the extreme Puritan beliefs of New Englanders. Still, the belief in witches, ghouls and hobgoblins was deeply rooted in the state, mainly within the greater context of folk beliefs of eighteenth-century New Jersey. Folkways— or rules that cover customary ways of thinking, feeling and behaving—lack moral overtones or significance. Dr. Jon M. Shepard of the University of Kentucky stated that because folkways are not considered vital to group welfare, disapproval of those who break them is not great. "Those who consistently violate folkways—say, by talking loudly in quiet places, wearing shorts with a suit coat and tie, [singing and dancing in the middle of the field at night]—may appear odd. We may avoid these people, but we do not consider them wicked or immoral."[65]

Many folkways and beliefs, including those in the supernatural, were brought over from European countries by New Jerseyans' ancestors. For the state's people, they were more "odd" than "dangerous" per se. As mentioned previously, the state was indeed ripe for such beliefs on account of its diverse population. By the beginning of the American Revolution in 1775, the population of New Jersey numbered 120,000, a significant rise from the mere 15,000 in 1702. About one-sixth of the population had its roots in Scotland, Ireland or Wales; another one-sixth were Dutch; one-tenth were German; perhaps as much as one-twelfth were from Africa; and small portions of the population were Swedish, French, Belgian and of other national stocks.[66] When examined in this context, the belief in ghosts and spirits and the ease with which Ransford Rogers was able to spin his web of deception becomes not so farfetched.

James West Davidson and Mark Hamilton Lytle's celebrated work *After the Fact: The Art of Historical Detection* provided a helpful blueprint when studying the beliefs in the supernatural within the historical context. In their analysis of the Salem Witch Trials, the historians acknowledged that when a historian who does not believe in the supernatural forces is studying a given topic in which witchcraft plays a role, they are entering a psychological world in which they are an outsider. "[They] may think it a simple matter to understand how a [Morristown resident from 1788] would behave, but people who hold beliefs foreign to our own do not often act the way that we think they should think."[67] Thus, the best we can do in this case is try to understand members of Morristown society and how they allowed themselves to be deceived by beliefs that, even at their time, were already becoming outdated and ridiculed. We can also assert that they knew as much themselves. To avoid embarrassment, they went to great lengths to erase any record of their ordeal for posterity. Hence, considering the 1700s New Jersey folk beliefs held by the participants, all that is left to understand is why they would feel compelled to be frightened by the imagined threat, even against their better judgment.

"Psychiatric research has long established what we now take for granted: that people may act for reasons they themselves do not fully understand, from motives buried deep within the unconscious."[68] The stories contained in this chapter detailing the various inflictions caused by supernatural powers and observed by the author of the infamous 1792 pamphlet, as well as the editors of the *Pennsylvania Gazette* and Reverend Tuttle, show a community with deep-rooted superstitions. These fantasies may not have been feared as much as scorned or even mocked, albeit still legitimately accepted by some people as facts of life, even if not universally followed. The fear that gripped both the first and second Companies was to them very real. As far as they were concerned, they were facing the scorn of a presumably evil force they could not defend themselves against. Together with the belief that Rogers was a spiritual being—a witch man of sorts—capable of protecting them against this danger that they could not fathom or escape from, one becomes a bit more empathetic of their fallacy.

Anthropologists who have studied and analyzed the belief in witchcraft and the supernatural within different historical contexts have arrived at a conclusion that might further explain the supposed gullibility of the Company. Namely, their studies reveal that fear arising from the belief in the supernatural can be traumatic enough to lead to death. While that would be a remarkable reaction, it is nonetheless possible to be that scared. "An Australian aborigine who discovers himself bewitched will stand aghast….He attempts to shriek but usually the sounds chokes in his throat….His body begins to tremble and the muscles twist involuntarily….He sways back and forth and falls to the ground, foaming at the mouth; eventually, the victim refuses to eat, loses interest in life, and dies."[69] Davidson and Lythe compare this phenomenon to the neurological syndrome psychologists refer to as conversion hysteria. While normally, a nervous person deals with their emotions through conscious action or thought, when those ordinary means of coping fail, the unconscious takes over.[70] "Hysterical patients will convert their mental worries into physical symptoms, such as blindness, paralysis of various parts of the body, choking, fainting or attacks of pain, [none which can be traced to organic causes]."[71] As such, the best way to explain it is this: Ransford Rogers managed to instill such fear in his subjects as to make it debilitating enough for them to think it impossible to survive without his help.

The area was primed for Ransford to carry out his scheme successfully, especially considering the already present superstitions of the 1700s American backcountry and the less educated lifestyle and folkloric beliefs of its citizens. In a sense, he did not bring anything new to the table but simply played off already present delusions. Furthermore, there is the unavoidable fact that he was initially sought out by some locals from the area and not the other way around. Rogers did not move to New Jersey until he was more or less contracted to help counter the spirits guarding the treasure. Once in Morristown, he played up the concerns of a few citizens before seeing the potential in the con and turning to the recruitment of new individuals. Still, at the end of the day, Ransford Rogers was only successful in his scheme because the sociological climate and culture of the area at the time allowed him to be so. And in the simplest terms, he managed to see his con nearly to the end because he scared his subjects stiff.

CONS, CRIMES AND
MORRIS COUNTY

T he people of Morristown, the center of prosperous and historically
significant Morris County in the state of New Jersey, were unfortunately
predisposed to be swindled. To fully comprehend the success with which
Ransford Rogers was able to commit his con and to understand the reason
why so much work has gone into covering up any names of those implicated
in the crime of ignorance and credulousness, we must examine another
con, a scam considered a "foul blemish upon [Morris County's] local
history, bringing disgrace to the town [of Morristown] and sorrow of heart
to the estimable family of which [the perpetrator] was a most unworthy
representative."[72] In fact, the counterfeiting scheme, which occurred over
a decade before Rogers began his own con, thrust not only one of Morris
County's most prominent families into the spotlight but also the entirety
of Morris County. The people of Morristown swore that they would never
again allow themselves to be smeared all over the state's papers as backward
people, gullible enough to be scammed by one of their own.

The family of the person responsible suffered greatly upon discovering
their son's involvement in the scam, and any repetition of the event, or one
like it, needed to be stifled before it inflicted such damage again. It is most
likely because of this earlier event that we never learned the specific names
of those involved in the story of the Morristown Ghost. As the saying goes,
fool me once, shame on you; fool me twice, shame on me. The details of
the story of Ransford Rogers were perpetually hidden and/or purposely
ignored in all subsequent histories of the county as not to further slander the

prominent family names of the individuals involved. It is very likely because of the counterfeiting scam that the true story of the 1788 con took on the appearance of a local legend and a ghost story and has been presented as such in various collections about the state's stories ever since.

The seriousness of the counterfeiting sting of 1768 is probably best summarized by the intensity with which it was presented by the editors of the first history of its kind, *The History of Morris County, New Jersey*. "It is not surprising that there should be at least one blot about the fair history of Morristown. We would fain pass it by, but the truth is inexorable, and the historian has no choice." In fact, as opposed to the anonymous pamphlet lacking any substantial evidence as to the names of those involved, the names and details of those who partook in the money scam were already reported on. Thus, while the editors of the county's first official written history could not hide that which was already in plain sight, they could at least ensure that any more disgrace pointed at the area and its people would not see the light of day. Historians of the time and even those who wrote about these events one hundred years later were more than OK with the story of the Morristown Con of 1788 being placed alongside local legends, such as that of the New Jersey Devil, further distancing it from reality. The following is an account of the earlier con, which likely served as the impetus for the secrecy of the Morristown Ghost pamphlet that followed a few short years later. Unless otherwise noted in the endnotes, the following account comes from *The History of Morris County, New Jersey*, as well as Reverend Joseph F. Tuttle's *The Early History of Morris County, New Jersey*, which was read before the New Jersey Historical Society on May 20, 1869, and *The Proceedings of the New Jersey Historical Society*, second series, vol. 4., *1875–1877*, printed in Newark in 1877.

The counterfeiting con, pleasantly called a "money-making affair" by its main culprit and leader of the notorious gang of counterfeiters, Samuel Ford, was orchestrated by members of the most prominent and respectable families from Morris County. In fact, the names of the people involved can still be heard in the area today, over two centuries later, namely on street signs, local historical markers and/or businesses' advertisements. The young Ford was a grandson of a widow, Elizabeth Lindsley, the mother of Colonel Jacob Ford, whose house became George Washington's headquarters during

The Ford Cottage built by Gabriel Ford Jr., the grandson of Colonel Jacob Ford Sr., one of Morristown's wealthiest citizens and a relation of Samuel Ford. *Photograph by the author.*

the winter of 1779–80. Today, the house is noted for being one of the earliest house museums in the United States. His accomplices in villainy also came from what would be considered high society by the time's standards. They were Benjamin Cooper of Hibernia, today's Rockaway, the son of Judge Cooper, before whom he was afterward tried for his crime; Dr. Bern Budd, a leading physician in Morristown; Samuel Hanes and one Ayers of the Denville Rockway area, both prominent members of society, with one also being a justice of the peace; and, last but not least, David Reynolds, a common man with no strong social connections.[73] Samuel Ford's first wife also went by the name of Kitchell; today, this family name graces various street signs and even a lake in the state of New Jersey.

Before beginning his operations in Morris County, Samuel Ford was already arrested on charges of counterfeiting in 1768 in New York, where he was caught trying to pass fake New Jersey bills of credit. As the story goes, he then left his first wife, and before being brought to trial, he escaped to Ireland, where he improved his skills. Ireland was reputed to furnish, at this time, the most skillful counterfeiters in the world.[74] Upon returning to the states in 1772, Ford settled in a small cabin hideout that was deadlocked within a swampy area between Morristown and Hanover. With his base of operations all set, he officially moved back to Morristown to begin the greatest con of the county's short history—at least until the Morristown Ghost. Day after day, Ford would leave his home at daylight with his gun, as to give off the appearance of going hunting; he would then make his way to his secret hideout. This was not viewed as suspicious by his neighbors, who simply saw this as being in line with the young man's laid-back and idle lifestyle. Once he was near his hidden cabin, Ford would creep on his hands and knees to avoid being seen in the open landscape. This was by no means a pleasant endeavor, as, for the greater part of the year, the water surrounding his hideout was a foot deep

Yet, as seems to be the case with many individuals who fall into scamming or robbing others for their gain, Samuel Ford was not smart enough to curtail his spending of the questionably acquired loot. It was difficult for people to understand how a man whose only ostensible means of livelihood were a few acres of swampy land, the cultivation of which was sadly neglected, could wear the aspect of a thriving farmer with plenty of money.[75] With many questions swarming around his persona, he was finally called out by one of his neighbors, who reported him to a local judge. That fateful day came on July 16, 1773, when Ford was finally arrested and lodged in the Morris County Jail. His stay was, however, short-lived. The man known simply as Sam to those who knew him was nowhere to be found the morning after his arrest when a constable checked in on him and brought him breakfast. It is believed that Ford was assisted in his escape by one John King. Examining the files of the county jail from the time, one is made to think that this is the same John King who was, at the time of the escape, an under sheriff of Morris County. Fortunately for John, it was not him but the county's head sheriff Mr. Kinney who was later indicted for carelessness in the line of duty to allow the dangerous prisoner to escape unobstructed. The privy council regarded him as "blamable for negligence in his office, respecting the escape of Ford" and advised the governor "to prosecute said indictment at the next court case."[76]

As for Sam, the master counterfeiter escaped into hiding in the mountain range of today's Rockway Township, New Jersey, somewhere between Mount Hope and Hibernia, presumably near today's Hawk Watch at Wildcat Ridge Wildlife Management Area in Morris County. According to another account by Reverend Joseph F. Tuttle, in his *The Early History of Morris County, New Jersey*, Ford chose the Hibernia location, as he once co-owned a horse pound and ironworks in the area with one of his coconspirators, Benjamin Cooper. According to a statement from his niece Mrs. Eunice Pierson, when in hiding at Hibernia after his escape, Sam settled in a deserted colliery called "Smultz's Cabin," from which he was nearly caught.[77] Based on the research of Reverend Tuttle, a fourteen-year-old James Kitchell of the Rockway/ Denville area was present at the Rockway Meeting House on the Sunday that Sheriff Kinney arrested Abraham Kitchell and forced to be a guide for the posse to find Ford's hiding place in the mountains. "The greatly excited boy ran home, but on the way stopped to tell one John Herriman of the occurrence."[78] Apparently, the latter hastily dressed and ran over the meadows for Hibernia to warn Ford. Possibly to evoke some feelings of doubt toward the legitimacy and true intentions of the men responsible for finding Ford—or to perhaps let/help him escape—the sheriff took the matter unhurried, according to Reverend Tuttle's research. This was after Mr. Kitchell, his guide, said to him publicly, "'I know where Ford is, and will take you to the sport, but you know you dare not, for your own sake, arrest him!' At last, at a leisurely pace, they searched the cabin, and sure enough, Ford was gone. 'There, sheriff,' said Kitchell as they entered the cabin, 'is where Sam Ford has been secreted, and you would rather give your horse, saddle and bridle than to find him here now!'"[79] The sheriff was duly relieved of his post by the privy council within weeks for his supposed botched attempt at capturing the criminal.

There is some merit to the assumption that there was more to the tale and perhaps more people involved than what was initially recorded by history. According to the files of the *Pennsylvania Gazette* from 1773, which can be accessed on the commercial website and subsidiary of Ancestry. com, Newspapers.com, it took a dubious amount of time to discover Ford's hideout in the Hibernia Mountains of Rockway. Analyzed alongside New York's *Rivington's Gazette*, which Reverend Tuttle previously evaluated, it becomes apparent that there was no haste on the part of the sheriff to find the infamous criminal. Looking at the dates, Sam escaped from the county jail on July 18 and was known to have been hiding in nearby Hibernia from that point on until at least late September. Yet Sheriff Kinney did not publish the offer of reward money for the criminal until August 5 in the *Rivington Gazette* and September 22 in the *Pennsylvania Gazette*.[80]

As for Samuel Ford, it appears that his pursuit after the second escape was not much better than his initial hunt. The master counterfeiter had escaped to Green Brier County in the mountains of Virginia, where he took on his mother's maiden name of Baldwin and started a new family. He gave up his

The Morristown Green marker, where the courthouse that held the cases of Samuel Ford and later Ransford Rogers once stood. *Photograph by the author.*

ways and instead turned his interests toward becoming a silversmith, which he allegedly turned into great wealth and property. Even when his whereabouts became known back home, it did not seem that he was in any way sought out for his earlier crimes. His eldest son, William Ford, visited him in Virginia, where he found his father to be a quiet and religious man who had settled down with his new bride and helped raise their young children. There is no record of the new Mr. Baldwin ever having to answer for his crimes. As for the counterfeiting scheme itself, after several other people were taken up on suspicion, they divulged the whereabouts of Ford's hideout and the details of the con. Ford's swamp was located, and upon examination, a printing press was found. The shack also contained a set of plates for printing bills of Maryland, Pennsylvania, New York and New Jersey; a quantity of type and other materials; and a leather wrapper in which the money was kept.[81] Long after Ford changed his name to Baldwin and was never seen or heard from again in New Jersey, another Morris County sheriff by the name of

Robinson purchased the home in which the Fords lived and, while repairing it, found some of Ford's counterfeiting tools in the walls, where, many years before, the con man had secretly hidden them.[82]

The point of the story that most relates to the latter Morristown Ghost Con of 1788 can be found in the aftermath of Ford's counterfeiting scheme—namely, the effect it had on those involved and their families. Samuel's family was left in dire straits after his escape to Virginia. According to Morris County court records from September 1773, Sheriff Kinney all but gave away Samuel Ford's farm in Hanover by naming it as part of a suit by one Benjamin Lindlsey, who found himself swindled by the infamous con man. Called the Hammock, the farm containing about 130 acres was the last thing and only livelihood that the escapee's family possessed. Because Ford did not appear in court as was demanded, his wife found herself with an order for her land to be sold by the next September court term (1774).[83] As the woman refused to yield, the appointed auditors allowed the abandoned wife to stay at least until the death of her and Sam's son, William. Once that fateful day came, the land was sold, and the older woman moved to a small home in Whippany, New Jersey, until her death. As for Ford's high-society coconspirators, their story unravels a very compelling argument about Morris County protecting its well-respected citizens—a point that becomes even more important when attempting to bring the story of the Morristown Ghost back into the realm of history.

After the men were taken on suspicion of playing a part in Ford's scheme, the papers soon began to list their names, revealing their high positions in society. There was no hiding from the accusations, as more and more evidence was being uncovered, including, in some cases, written correspondence between some of the men and Samuel. The confessions that Cooper, Haynes and Budd made under the gallows all revealed not only the counterfeiting con but also a great robbery. The *Pennsylvania Gazette* from September 29 reported that "Cooper [also] confessed himself privy to the robbery of the treasury at Amboy, and that he received £300 of the money; on which he also was respited till he should make further discoveries."[84] The article added that Cooper swore that the whole affair, including the robbery and the counterfeiting scheme, was planned "by Ford and perpetrated by him and three soldiers then quarantined there." The story also pointed to some conspirators being shocked by Samuel's one-time suggestion that they should blame an innocent man if caught. Ford apparently replied, "No, damn him, he will only be condemned, he has friends enough to save him from the gallows."[85] This is an ironic statement when placed in context of what ultimately happened to all his conspirators who were put on trial for treason. While there seems to be no doubt that Samuel Ford was indeed the ringleader, it still needs to be noted that a letter exists that challenges that assertion. Writing to Cooper after his escape, Ford berated his accuser for his "atrocious falsehood" in placing the blame solely on him for the robbery at the treasury at Perth Amboy and the counterfeiting con. "You describe me as being the chiefest promoter and first introducer of the money-making affair," he stated, adding, "Did you not in time of our distressed circumstances at [Hibernia] first move this scheme to me?"[86] The letter and its contents, however, would not aid or hinder the fate of his conspirators. It would be their social standing that would play a much larger role in deciding their fates.

The arraignment took place in the old courthouse in Morristown on August 19, 1773 (the old courthouse was located on today's Morristown Green and was where the Morristown Ghost Trial was heard). "A thousand people were thought to be within its walls, and among them all, scarcely an eye could be found which did not exhibit some token of sympathetic sorrow."[87] According to the *Pennsylvania Gazette*, "Reynolds, Haynes, Cooper and Budd were tried, confessed their guilt and were condemned to be hanged. Their execution was ordered for the 17th [of September]."[88] Yet it was not to be. Morristown and Morris County take care of their own—at least those with a certain social position. As reported in *The History of Morris County*, not only was one of the magistrates before whom the case was tried the father of one of the culprits but "the best families and society in the county had representatives in the number of the condemned." It was the respectability of the culprits, as well as their influential connections, *The History of Morris County* asserts, that had the greatest effect on the pardoning power. "The day fixed for their execution arrived, and Reynolds, who seemed to have been really the least guilty of the lot but who alone, unfortunately for himself, had no influential friends, suffered the ignominious death to which he had been sentenced; while the other three were remanded, and finally, in December, after a number of respites, [the governor] gave them a full pardon."[89] The men continued to live within the county unmolested and, one might even say, protected by their neighbors.

Twentieth-century historian John L. Brooke suggested that the sequence of events in Morris County, New Jersey, typified the relationship between divining and counterfeiting. "Involving mutual assistance among noted families and the connivance of justices of the peace, constables and a church deacon, the counterfeiting conspiracy must have created a paranoiac sense

The Morristown Green, where the courthouse once stood that held the Ford case in 1773 and later that of Ransford Rogers in front of the honorable Judge Gabriel Hogarth Ford. *Photograph by the author.*

of anxiety and distrust."[90] He further added that establishing a copper penny mint in Morristown in 1786 might have also fed local speculation on the creation of wealth. Together with the already mentioned beliefs of the supernatural reported in the area, Brooke believed that the people of Morris County were predisposed for the reception of Ransford Rogers and his con. All of this resulted in the form of a belief in a treasure being buried in nearby Schooler's Mountain. And since Rogers seemed like the man who could help them gain this wealth, what he said had to be true. As such, Brooke's sequence is quite simple: the operations of counterfeiters created an environment of anxiety about deceptions by mysterious powers and a fascination with easy wealth, both of which, in turn, fed a belief in witchcraft and treasure fantasies.[91]

The inclusion of the story of this con within these pages serves a dual purpose. First, it showcases the desire of the people of Morristown to take attention away from the area's already tainted history. Between the terrible treatment of Loyalists during the Revolutionary War, the local-interest-transcending robbery of the East Jersey Treasury at Perth Amboy and the subsequent money counterfeiting scheme that mostly affected the county's locals, Morristown and Morris County as a whole knew they could not afford another blemish on their character. Also, the subsequent court case following the unraveling of Ford's con points to an even greater connection to the story of the Morristown Ghost Con of 1788. It is very evident that the people of the area would go to great lengths to protect the respected members of society, even if that meant having a presumably innocent man take the blame and pay the ultimate price for a crime that other more noteworthy gentlemen committed. This is perhaps the biggest clue as to why the author of *The Morristown Ghost* (and the *Fac-Simile* copy) chose to not only remain anonymous but also did the same for the names of all those involved when putting ink to paper. Unknown to them, in doing so, they became one of the main reasons historians mostly ignored the story, and it subsequently fell into the realm of fables. At least now, nearly two and a half centuries later, we can assert the impetus for the author's choice and help the story of the Morristown Ghost become history once more— or perhaps, for the first time.

HISTORY'S SEARCH
FOR RANSFORD ROGERS

W ho was Ransford Rogers? Was he capable of committing the crime?
One confirming bit of evidence are the legal records of Morris
County from 1789 to 1790, which show Rogers's indictment for fraud and
conspiracy, his bail jumping and the division of the property he left behind
among his creditors.[92] At this trial, the presiding justice of the peace was
one Gabriel Hogarth Ford of the famous Ford family, who were previously
involved in the counterfeiting scheme of few years prior. Undeniably,
Ransford Rogers was indeed a real person and a real con man. Most
important are the independent accounts detailing his wicked career after
his escape from Morristown. Over the years, his name appears in the local
histories and papers from Pennsylvania, New England and throughout the
South. In each place, the "Morristown Ghost" ran a variant of his treasure
scam.[93] Morristown, it appears, was a place where the man simply honed his
skills. Thus, the story of the Morristown Ghost, or the Morris County Con
of 1788, is perhaps just an introduction to the more extensive history of a
con man who operated in the United States' Atlantic region around the turn
of the nineteenth century.

We do not know much about Ransford's upbringing, but what we do
know might shed some light on his belief and choice to carry out a con in
his adult life. Born in the New London region of Connecticut, Ransford
was still a mere child when his father, Joseph Rogers, died in 1763. His
father was a great-nephew of none other than John Rogers, the founder of
the Rogerene Quakers, a religious sect in Connecticut. Thus, he was also

related to his daughter Bathsheba Fox, who put witch puppets in the New London meetinghouse in 1694.[94] The Rogerenes advocated toleration and a separation between church and state—a problematic proposition in light of Connecticut's stance on conforming to a state-sanctioned religion. When Rogerenes refused to pay a minister's rate or tax in support of a corrupt ministry, authorities satisfied the rate through criminal prosecutions, fines and confiscations.[95] What the Rogerene are most known for in New England history is their stance on the Sabbath. "Not wanting to correct the errors of their congressional neighbors, citing God—who 'spoke' directly through the body of their leader—as their ultimate authority; the group worshiped any day of the week and at any location, but on Sundays. While the colony gathered in meetinghouses all day, Rogerenes openly flouted the law by putting themselves to work, often at menial labor."[96] It may have been his upbringing and un-Protestant beliefs about one's relationship toward established religion that made Rogers seek out respectable Protestant church members as the targets of his second con. However, this does not explain his initial choice of the prominent members of society, regardless of their church affiliations—except, of course for their presumed wealth. In the least, Rogers's upbringing provides us with a glimpse into his possible predisposition toward questioning authority and those in power.

Ransford's story between his early years and his eventual appearance in Morristown at the request of two locals is nonexistent. We know that once he arrived in Morris County, he opened a schoolhouse about three miles west of Morristown proper. Based on surviving accounts from the 1800s, collected by various historians for the *Historical Magazine*, edited by Henry B. Dawson, we know a little more about Rogers's time in New Jersey. Based on interviews with locals who were alive to remember the events of his scheme, we know that Rogers taught in the area for several months to the great satisfaction of his patrons. He was known to have been very "enterprising… and had the faculty of keeping his scholars excited in their studies."[97] In an interview conducted in the 1850s by historian Reverend Joseph F. Tuttle, DD, an older gentleman recalled how "Rogers frequently held exhibitions of his school, in the barn of Mr. Hedges. Declamations and dialogues formed the entertainment, and these were of a kind so rude that it was a wonder that they did not make the horse break their halters!" The old man added, "The people were very predisposed for his reception and fond of the numerous exhibitions, which he was able to perform with surprising dexterity." No one, with the exception of the two men who brought Rogers to the area, knew or suspected the real reason he was charming—or, might we say, bewitching—the population of Morristown.

Following his escape from Morris County after the conclusion of his second con, Ransford seemed to disappear from the annals of history, at least for a while. During that time, the con man changed his name and identity. This seemed to be a habit with each new place he visited. At one point, he even managed to get married. While there are cases of similar cons being committed throughout the South, with many attributed to the man formerly known as Ransford Rogers, the newspapers that make the claims never provide enough details or record the events enough to confirm that it was indeed the work of Rogers. There is, however, one case that did make the local newspaper. More importantly, it is detailed enough to make the probability almost certain that the main culprit is none other than Ransford Rogers. Ironically, while the narrative acknowledges that the people conned by "a ghost" were the most respected members of that society, it does not shy away from providing all their names.

Written by the honorable Judge John Henry of York County, Pennsylvania, who presided over the case of Ranford's second con, the account not only resurrects Ransford Rogers from anonymity but also provides us with the context of what he was up to in the years immediately after he left Morristown. Reprinted in the *Lancaster Examiner* in October 1912, Henry's notes begin with "Rice Williams, or rather Ransford Rogers, a New Englander, and John Hall, a New Yorker—both of whom had been plundering the inhabitants of the southern states by their wiles—arriving at the house of Clayton Chamberlain, a neighbor of [John] Dady, in July 1797."[98] Upon further examination of the similarity of the events that transpired in Pennsylvania to those in Morristown seven years prior, we can confidently say that Ransford Rogers's career as a supernatural con man—and thus, the Morristown Ghost Con itself—were nothing short of factual.

Rice Williams's (Roger Ransford's) main assistant in the York County Ghost Con was Dr. John Dady, a German-born, one-time Hessian who came to the area during the Revolutionary War and chose to settle on the border of York and Adams Counties in Pennsylvania. The narrative, taken by Judge Henry from the accounts of those accused as well as those swindled, begins with Dady's neighbor one Clayton Chamberlain. Introduced by Dady, Ransford and his fellow traveler John Hall sat down with Clayton and asked him if his house was haunted. After being told no, Rogers informed the man that it was, as "I have been born with a veil over my face and can see spirits…and have been conducted thither, sixty miles, by a spirit." Sitting quietly up to this point, Hall interjected that what Ransford was saying was indeed true. Trusting the good-natured Dr. Dady, who also corroborated the mysterious travelers' story, Clayton agreed to meet them in the field that evening, where Rogers would show him the spirit that had guided him to Chamberlain's home. What follows, while slightly different, is too similar to the Morristown events to be a coincidence.

It was midnight on a pleasantly warm summer evening when the men assembled in the lonely field. The still skeptical Chamberlain agreed to show up but was in no hurry, as he arrived later than was agreed upon. Williams, the name Rogers then went by, told the men to step back as he drew a circle on the ground. He then directed Hall and Clayton to walk in silence around the circle. Peculiarly, John Dady, who insisted Chamberlain come, was nowhere to be seen. As the two men walked in silence, "a terrible screech was soon heard, proceeding from a 'Black Ghost' at a distance from the parties in the direction opposite to the place where Williams stood." The Black Ghost, it was explained, was the bad spirit that was trying to prevent a white spirit from carrying out its mission. As if on cue, a White Ghost appeared in the distance, presumably Dady wearing a white sheet. Williams spoke to this spirit "in a language which those who heard him could not understand and the ghost replying in the same language!" After the apparition had gone, and with Chamberlain now visibly shaken, Williams proceeded to disclose that the White Ghost called him to Clayton's farm because he knew of a treasure that was permitted to be discovered by eleven men. Those men, the spirit proclaimed, had to be honest, religious and sensible and neither horse jockeys nor Irishmen. With his mouth open, all Chamberlain could do was nod his head in silent agreement.

Dady was never seen alongside Rogers (or Williams) as not to arouse any suspicion from that point forward. As for Chamberlain, who was then fully convinced of the existence of a ghost and a hidden treasure, the man set off to form a new company. Judge Henry later reported at the trail of John Dady that each candidate was initiated by the receipt of a small, sealed paper containing a little bit of yellow sand that was called "the power." After receiving the package from Williams, each man was instructed to bury it in the earth exactly one inch deep for three days and three nights. During this time, they had to perform "several absurd ceremonies," to which the Honorable Henry proclaimed they were "too obscene to be described [at the trial]." Once selected, the men proceeded to meet in the same field that turned Chamberlain into a believer. A new circle was formed, in the center of which was a hole that was six inches wide and six inches deep. A captain, a lieutenant and three committeemen were elected, with Hall getting the top job. The men then paced around the circle, which they were told would propitiate and strengthen the White Ghost. On several occasions, they were prompted to walk faster when the apparition of the Black Ghost appeared with loud bellows and sometimes rocks being thrown at them from different directions.

On the night of August 18, 1797, Williams asked the men to stop walking as he took a sheet of clean white paper and folded it in the form of a letter. He then asked each member to breathe into it three times; "this being repeated several times and the paper laid over the hole in the center of a circle, the instructions of the ghost were obtained." The paper was very blunt with its message.

> *Go on, and do right, and prosper, and the treasure shall be yours. I am permitted to write this in the same hand I wrote in the flesh for your direction.... Take care of your powers in the name and fear of God, our protector—if not, leave the work. There is a great treasure, £4,000 apiece for you. Don't trust the Black One. Obey orders. Break the enchantment, which you will not do until you get an ounce of mineral dulcimer eliximer; some German doctors have it. It is near, and dear, and scarce. Let the committee get it—but don't let the doctor know what you are about—he is wicked.*

So Dady's role in the con began wholeheartedly, all under the guise of being ignorant of the scheme. A few days later, he was met by a young man named Abraham Kephart, whom the committee chose to procure the elixir from the good German doctor. Dady mixed the "eliximer" in a small bottle, sealed with a large red seal and buried it in a heap of oats. After demanding $15 for his concoction, which the young man could not pay, the doctor told him to summon someone who could, as this elixir was very rare and expensive. By the end of the week, one committeeman gave Dady $36 and three bushels of oats for three ounces of the elixir. Another, one Yost Liner, gave the doctor $121 for eleven ounces.[99]

In the words of the indictment that eventually followed, the men involved were "most miserably duped," as well as "cheated and defrauded by means of certain false tokens and pretenses, to wit, by means of pretended spirits, certain circles, certain brown powder, and certain compositions called mineral dulcimer elixir or Deterick's mineral elixir." While there is no purpose of listing the names of those involved here, they can all be found by examining the *Lancaster Examiner* from October 9, 1912. The same article also mentions that the con men did not stop there but were able to trick a total of thirty-nine people in their ghostly schemes. Before the initial con was even finished, the plotters moved on to nearby Shrewsbury Township, also in Pennsylvania, about forty miles away from Dr. Dady's home. A man named Jacob Wister, one of the new batch of conspirators, acted as Rogers's agent. This time, his scheme was able to bring together over twenty individuals, "all of whom were, of course, most ignorant people." The same ceremonies as those carried out in the other scam were performed. Although not specified, it was noted that "the communications of the ghost were obtained in a still more ridiculous manner than before."

Once more, the communication specifically singled out Dr. Dady as the person from whom the Company should procure the dulcimer elixir. This time, the quasi-sand mixture was referred to as "Asiatic Sand" and was one again necessary to give efficiency to the so-called powers. Ulrich Neaff, a committeeman of this second Company, paid Dady ninety dollars for seven and a half ounces of the secret concoction. The substance was placed inside small vials, which were brought to the remote nightly meeting places. Those could then be seen in the hands of the Company, as the men shook them while prancing around the circle. On certain occasions, they anointed the tops of their heads with them. Only after the ritual and upon further direction from the White Ghost would the men go off to burry the elixir in the ground, all while counting down the days until they would be led to a hidden treasure.

Just as he exhibited years before in New Jersey, Ransford Rogers was unable to put aside his greed and walk away at the right time. As reported in the court documents months later, the good fraternity began to break within the group of con men due to Rogers's ravenous actions. Another of the committeemen, Paul Baliter, went to visit Dr. Dady's office with one hundred dollars of his family's savings. When he failed to find Dady at home, he was met by Williams (Rogers), who happily obtained as much desired sand as Baliter's money could buy. The issue was laid with the fact that the master con man never told the good doctor of the transaction and instead kept the money for himself. Yet before Dady even found out, Ransford, as he did in Morristown before, wanted to make even more money for himself, regardless of the fact that everything around him was telling him that he should pack up and move, especially before the men became suspicious that the lofty purchases of the elixir were not bringing them any closer to a hidden treasure. What followed lets us in on the fact that Ransford had at some point married, with his wife playing a part in his last con and ultimately his undoing.

Having realized that he did not need Dr. Dady, the master con man decided to make up a fictitious doctor to whom the company should go to for the elixir. This new doctor was John Huber, none other than Ransford Rogers himself. In preparation, the next time the two Companies met, Ransford procured directions from his ghost that each of the Companies should dispatch a committeeman to Lancaster to buy "Dederick's Mineral Elixer" from a German physician in that place. As reported later, at this time, Ransford and his wife, Mrs. Williams, hurried to Lancaster, where they prepared the elixir, "which was nothing but a composition of copperas and cayenne pepper." But there was one hiccup that the couple did not foresee. Lancaster already had one German doctor, Dr. Rose. As Ransford did not specify which German doctor to see when the committeemen made their way to the town, he and his wife needed to act quickly. Mrs. Williams, acting as the wife of one John Huber, a new German doctor in town, went to Dr. Rose with a letter that stated they had moved, "thirteen miles from Newcastle, Delaware," which directed him on how to sell the new article that she had brought him. He was asked to hold onto the new drug until her husband could open his office in a few weeks' time. The older gentleman found this to be odd but agreed to sell the medicine in their name. Undeniably, he doubted anyone would even know to ask for it. Mrs. Williams thanked the man and told him she would come back at the end of the week to collect any money that might have been secured from the sale of the "medicine." All would have worked if the enormity of the price the lady had set for the concoction was not so high as to arouse the suspicions of the old doctor. The more he thought about it, it just did not seem right to him.

To the doctor's massive surprise, within a few days, people began to show up asking for the mysterious elixir. Within a week, the delegates from the committees had left behind $740.33 from purchasing the potion blend. Not wanting to be involved in what seemed to him like criminal activity, the doctor contacted the authorities. When the lady came for the money, she was restrained and arrested. Within hours, the secret was out. As detailed by the honorable Judge John J. Henry, an indictment was presented in the Criminal Court of York County against Dr. John Dandy, Rice Williams, Hesse Miller, Jacob Wister, the elder, and Jacob Wister, the younger, for conspiracy to cheat and defraud. The trial took place the next June and resulted in the conviction of Wister, the elder, and Dr. Dady (the former was fined $10 and imprisoned one month in the county jail; the latter was fined $90 and sentenced to two years' confinement in the penitentiary in Philadelphia).[100] Dady had also been convicted of participating in the conspiracy in Shrewsbury, where he and Hall were found guilty of a similar crime in Adams County, whereupon Hall was fined $100 and sent to the penitentiary for two years and Dady was fined another $160 and sentenced to undergo an additional servitude of two years in the penitentiary, which was to commence in June 1800, when his first term would expire.[101]

As for Dr. John Huber, Rice Williams and Ransford Rogers, according to his wife, Rogers was waiting outside for her when she went into Dr. Rose's office to collect the money. Having witnessed his wife being captured, the one-time Morristown Ghost abandoned his wife and escaped. He was never heard from again and is presumed lost in any further annals of history. Still, with his penchant for changing names and reinventing himself, it would be ignorant to assume the man did not eventually settle down somewhere and live out his remaining years in peace. The Pennsylvania cons are very similar to Morristown's. They also show that Ransford Rogers did not learn a lesson from his time in Morris County. As in the earlier case, the York County swindles again showed his greed leading him toward the ultimate discovery and failure. One peculiar aspect of the case that is missing from these new instances was the local people's impetus for the belief that a treasure existed. York County was not the hotbed of Loyalist activity that Morris County was, nor was the war itself present in York County as much as it was in Morris County. Yet if not for anything else, the events that transpired in William Penn's one-time Poor Man's Paradise further solidified the validity of the story of the Morristown Ghost.

HISTORY'S SEARCH
FOR ROGERS'S "COMPANY"

Although many of the facts and characters present in the story of Rogers's Morristown Con of 1788 have purposely been omitted from the original tale, that does not mean it would be a lost cause to try to uncover some of them. Beginning with Reverend Tuttle's primary research into the story from the mid-nineteenth century and carrying over to historian Andrew Sherman's account in his *Historic Morristown, New Jersey: The Story of Its First Century*, there are enough hints available to reconstruct the factual series of events, locations and, in some cases, names of those involved. And while many of the buildings and areas described in the story no longer exist, some of the pieces uncovered point us to the general vicinity of where the events of the Morristown Ghost con actually took place. While the secrecy of the event was self-prescribed by the original historians from the area and the time, over the years, it became a necessity for those who followed. In the plainest terms, there was not enough proper evidence left for them to refer to. Today, the secrecy that was initially sought is no longer required. Yet uncovering some of these long-buried mysteries proves to be difficult due to the nature of the original historical artifacts that were left for us to analyze. That does not mean we cannot try to piece together some of the more factual details about Ransford's Company and the events that transpired in Morris County between 1788 and 1790.

From Reverend Tuttle's work, which was based on extensive interviews of those who knew the men involved in the original con, we gather—albeit fragmented—some important facts that help us fill in some gaps. We know that the first company met at "L———'s" house in "Solitude," and eight men were present. The entire affair was conducted with "the greatest secrecy," and Rogers impressed the whole party with a sense of his piety by having the meeting conducted on religious principles. With only the first letter of the Company man's name available, we turn to the other information we know—"Solitude." According to various records, the area that at the time was known as Solitude was situated on the left side of the road that is called Sussex Avenue today, about a mile and a half north of the Morristown Green, or "as one goes toward Mount Freedom," today's Randolph, Morris County. From *A History of Old Wheatsheaf Farm, Formerly "Solitude"*, we learn that the area was about one hundred acres of uncleared, mostly dense woodland. In the center was a house known as Solitude, which was built around 1737. It was considered a relatively large residence surrounded by fertile maize and wheat fields, and due to it being the only home built in the only clearing for miles, it was christened Solitude.[102] The land changed hands once during the time in question, and eventually, Solitude became an inn or tavern, and "its name, doubtless because of its fertile fields of wheat, which relative to the size of other clearings, was distinguishingly large, was changed to 'Wheatsheaf Inn' or, quite possibly, as shown by certain historical documents, "Wheatsheaf Tavern."[103]

While the "L" is somewhat misleading, we do know from the pamphlet itself and Mr. Tuttle's interviews that at least two of the more prominent members of the group duped by Rogers were justices of the peace. We also know that another was approached but declined. Correlating this evidence with Solitude as the meetinghouse, we come across the following, "Soon after the commencement of the Revolution, there removed to Morristown a man who subsequently became prominent in the county, state and national affairs and who, in the struggle of freedom, rendered most excellent service." His name was John Cleves Symmes. He was a delegate to the Continental Congress from New Jersey, the eventual father-in-law of President William Henry Harrison and one of the founding pioneers of the Northwest Territories. We also know that he purchased the home and the land known as Solitude in the 1770s and resided there until around 1788, when he requested to purchase one million acres in Ohio from the U.S. Congress in what became known as the Symmes Purchase. Historical records reveal that the purchase of the Northwest lands was not completed until October 15, 1788; therefore it is very possible that he still owned the house and the land known to all as Solitude around the time of the con.[104]

John Cleves Symmes

The site of a silver mine on the Old Judge Symmes Place, Morristown. *Courtesy of the Morris County Historical Society.*

Some accounts do have him moving out of the area in late 1787, but no definite date for this exists. What we know is that he relocated to Ohio between the years 1787 and 1789, initially part time and eventually permanently. Perhaps most interesting to this analysis is the fact that following the War for Independence, sometime between 1781 and 1783, Mr. Symmes resigned from the militia service and became a justice of the New Jersey Supreme Court. "It was while Mr. Symmes was a Justice of the Supreme Court of New Jersey, that the trial of 'Parson Caldwell's' murder occurred; and the writer [Andrew Sherman, 1905,] had seen the statement that during the famous trial, Justice Symmes presided over the court," proving his profession at least at one point being that of a justice of the peace. James Caldwell, who was stationed in Morristown during the Revolutionary War, was killed on November 24, 1781, by an American sentry, one James Morgan, when he refused to allow Morgan to inspect a package in his possession. The sentry was later hanged for the murder in 1782, as evidence came to light that suggested he was bribed to kill Caldwell, who was an ardent Presbyterian minister and Patriot. Piecing this together, we know that the Honorable J.C. Symmes was a justice of the peace. We also know that he lived at Solitude, one of the singled-out meeting places of the Company during/around the years of the swindle.

Still, by the time of the events pertaining to the Morristown Ghost scam, the land in question was going through somewhat of a transition. Sometime around the 1780s, one Walter Mould and his family moved to Morristown, acquiring the farm and residence. He then promptly began the coinage of copper pennies in the sitting room's fireplace. While records show that he had operated in Morris County since 1781, the specific year he acquired Solitude and turned it into a tavern as well as a mine where cooper was made into pennies is not known. It is believed to have happened sometime around 1788 or shortly thereafter, as that is when Judge Symmes seems to have vacated the premises. Thus, while it may be a stretch to assume that one of the defrauded individuals was someone of the caliber of Justice John Cleves Symmes, the gathered evidence prevents us from completely ruling out the possibility. He could, of course, have been the person singled out by Tuttle as the justice of the peace that turned down the offer of the Morristown Ghost—yet that is also as good a guess as anyone's.

But there is always the proximity of Solitude to Ransford Rogers's schoolhouse to contend with. As discovered by Reverend Tuttle during his research, "As you [would go] westward, a little beyond the schoolhouse in which Rogers taught, you [would] see a road which [led] from the main road, in a north-east direction, along the foot of the mountain. It passed through a region so lonely and out of the way, that it was called Solitude." It was this place that the historian stated "was destined to be famous as a favorite resort of 'The Morristown Ghost.'"[105] It is also mentioned that, near this area, "lived a carpenter and farmer, a very worthy man, but of limited intelligence and a profound believer in witchcraft." Was this man Walter Mould? Perhaps we will never know. Nonetheless, if J.C. Symmes or someone of the same prominence and reputation was involved, it is no wonder that the town and its people chose to suppress the names of those involved.

Another person who is not revealed to us by the pamphlet and is only referred to as "Colonel B——— H———" by Reverend Tuttle was an individual who played one of the most prominent roles in the con. He was also assumed to have been the one who lost the most money in the process. Once again, through corroboration with various sources, we uncover that—with more certainty than Symmes—the person in question was Colonel Benoni Hathaway.

As you leave Morristown, by the Bridgestreet [Road], northward, just in the edge of town, a few roads east of the main road, on the side hill, you see the residence of Colonel B——— H———, who was a conspicuous character, in Morris County during the Revolutionary War. His father, B——— H——— and his brother J———, were both physicians—not very learned ones, but having considerable practice. The brother resided about four miles north of Morristown at Littleton [today, Morris Plains]. *Colonel H——— was an enthusiastic Patriot and fought like a lion at the Second Battle of Springfield. He once had charge of the magazine in Morristown and prepared cartridges for the army. He was a tanner and currier; and by the dint of industry and economy, had secured a valuable farm, which was on either side of the road, leaving Morristown to Speedwell* [the current border of Morris Plains and Morristown, where Speedwell Avenue eventually changes into Littleton Road]. *He was greatly esteemed in the community for his generosity, public spirit and good character; but he had one weakness, the result rather of education and bad associations than of natural superstition—from infancy, he had been trained to believe in all the fooleries of witchcraft. In this respect his brother J—— was like him. But for this folly, both were strong men; and in spite of this, they wielded a strong influence in the community. These brothers were among the earliest dupes of Rogers; and the colonel, the one first mentioned, not merely became the treasurer of the association, but one of the heaviest losers by the fraud.*[106]

Based on this evidence collected from firsthand witnesses and corroborating it alongside the names of the most prominent colonels who lived in this area, we come across Benoni Hathaway. After studying his military career and looking at his family tree, courtesy of Ancestry.com as well as Genealogy.com and research conducted by Ruth Hathaway Keightley, a genealogist from the Hathaway Family Association, there can be no doubt as to who Col. B—— H—— was.

As mentioned by the original pamphlet, apart from two justices of the peace, the Company included a well-respected colonel and two doctors. Through uncovering Hathaway, his father and brother, both doctors, we add three—perhaps four—more names to the mystery of the Morristown Ghost. According to the Hathaway Family Association genealogist, Benoni Hathaway (B—— H——) was born in Morristown on November 6, 1742, and died on April 18, 1823. He served in the Revolution, first as a captain in the New Jersey Militia under Colonel Jacob Ford and later as a lieutenant colonel, a position for which he had a pension of $120 a year. He was known to have distinguished himself at the Battle of Springfield, for which he was eventually called the colonel in charge of Ford Powder Mill, with authority to supervise the removal of powder for the troops.[107] His father, one Benjamin Hathaway (B—— H——), according to the record of the Presbyterian Church in Morristown, is regarded as the donor of the land on which the original Presbyterian Church in Morristown was built in 1742 (in 1816, the church donated part of the land to the town for what would become the town square, or the Morristown Green); he was also the first president of the board of trustees and perhaps the most revered man in the community at the time. The church records also refer to Benjamin Hathaway being a physician and innkeeper.[108] There is enough evidence to point to the fact that Benjamin Hathaway was one of the doctors duped by Rogers.

Subsequently, Benjamin's other son and Benoni's brother, Jonathan Hathaway (J—— H——), was the other physician in question.

The Ford Powder Mill that Colonel Hathaway was in charge of during the Revolutionary War. *Courtesy of the Morris County Historical Society.*

According to the *Rockaway Records of Morris County, N.J. Families*, published in 1902, Jonathan was a doctor and a dentist as well. The records contain a fascinating history that further adds to the potential motivation the older brother of Benoni might have had in joining his brother in believing in the Morristown Ghost.

> *About halfway between Rockaway and Morristown, on Littleton Road, lived Jonathan Hathaway. He owned "the Hathaway Forge" between his residence and Morris Plains....The healing powers of Dr. Jonathan Hathaway's...ointments and other medicines, became known far and wide. Those who had been afflicted for many years applied to him for relief and returned to their homes almost miraculously cured. We knew one of the patients, Daniel Holly, who lived at Stockholm. He had boasted that he had never known a sick day in his life, but in his later years and ulceration afflicted the sole of his foot, and not having the patience of Job to endure the pain, he applied to Dr. Hathaway for relief, a distance of about thirty miles. Holly...consented to have the remedies applied....In a few weeks, the result was accomplished.*[109]

The author would not go so far as to say that Dr. Jonathan dabbled in any dark arts, but based on the surviving accounts, it becomes apparent that there was a certain mystery about Dr. Jonathan Hathaway's remedies, and some believed they included some ancient secrets. The doctor's popularity in the area led him to acquire "a goodly number of dollars and a small farm." He was also "a liberal benefactor [in the area] to the end."[110]

Returning to Reverend Tuttle's work, we are granted further hints as to who was involved in the first Company, albeit not their full names. We also get to know a little more about the role of Colonel Hathaway and Doctors Hathaway, as well as some geographical markers and locations of the events that transpired in 1788–89.

> *South-east from Morristown was another very excellent man, one B——— L———, a justice of the peace, but trained to weakness which betrayed so many worthy persons into the power of designing rogues. About halfway from Morristown to Speedwell on the stream was another dupe, one D——— C———, the owner of a gristmill. In Hanover Township, one S———, a man of some means, bore a leading part in the ridiculous affair. He once spent a whole evening with Aaron Kitchell, one of the strongest men in the county—a member of Congress, afterward— endeavoring to get him to join "The Spirit Batch," as it was popularly called. With the greatest secrecy, he talked; but Kitchell was not to be duped. Colonel H——— [Hathaway] tried to convert Abraham Kitchell, a brother of Aaron; but he "gave H——— [Colonel Hathaway] a book, telling him to read that and it would convince him that it was all a hoax!" In the vicinity of Dover, was Squire B——— L———, a son-in-law of Doctor J——— H———, who came into the measure quite reluctantly and with no faith, whatever; but tradition says, he had shrewdness enough to come out of it richer that he went in.*[111]

Upon further investigation of the *Rockaway Records of Morris County, N.J.*, as well as church, cemetery and marriage records from Morristown, it appears that Dr. Hathaway's son-in-law and squire, B——— L———, and

Colonel Hathaway's house.
Courtesy of the Morris County Historical Society.

The view of the old cemetery behind the Presbyterian church. Many of the people involved in the con were buried there, including Benoni Hathaway and his father, Benjamin Hathaway. *Photograph by the author.*

the justice of the peace B——— L——— are the same person, Benjamin Lamson Esq.

Benjamin married Thankful Hathaway, the daughter of Jonathan and Lydia Hathaway, on May 9, 1786. They were both buried in Rockaway, New Jersey. Lamson was very well respected in the community, and apart from being a justice of the peace, he was also the elder of Rockaway Church. He eventually inherited a property south of Dover known as Pigeon Hill, today's Union Hill of Denville, New Jersey. From *Rockaway Records of Morris County, N.J.*, we learn enough information that confirms his identity.

> *As will be seen by the church records, the latter part of the last century and the first part of this, no stationed minister was at Rockaway Church, and if we consult the marriage records at Morristown, we would find that at this period a large of the marriage ceremonies were performed by the justice of the peace, generally spoken of as squire....Esq. Benjamin Lamson held that office at this period, and his finances must have been largely increased by the swains, young and old, in all this region around about.[112]*

With that, we can finally close the secret case of the second and last justice of the peace who was involved in Ransford Rogers's scam. As for D———— C————, the only person who owned a gristmill on Speedwell Avenue during those years was a man by the name David Carmichael. And while not much is known about him, what we can deduce certainly points to him being the last mysterious man in this story.

One Aaron Kitchell was ultimately not persuaded to join the Company, but the potential of him ever being involved sheds further light on the caliber of the people who were targeted by the Morristown Ghost scam. It was considered by Ransford to have been a great loss that they were unable to convince either of the wealthy Kitchell brothers to join their group.

> One significant fact I have, from good authority…at the earnest solicitation of Colonel [Hathaway], A———— K———— [Abraham Kitchell] was induced to attend one of these mysterious prayer meetings, when he would see enough to give him faith; but the dull headed spectator, when his friend [Hathaway] "produced a paper, on which was the figure of a hand drawn by the ghost himself," declared that "any boy, or ordinary parts, or any old woman could draw one as good!" After the meeting, Rogers, who was not present, asked whether this man, K———— [Kitchell], had joined them; and when told that he had not, he asked, "Did you treat him? [Did you give him alcohol?]" "Yes, before he left." "There's the mistake," said Rogers, "You ought to have treated him when he first came so that whilst the prayers were going on, the spirits might have been at work in him to rase his ideas."[113]

So the Kitchell brothers got away but not before ridiculing those who chose to remain. Curiously, the two men—with at least Abraham seeing one of the meetings firsthand—knew of the shenanigans going on between some of the most prominent members of their society and this "ghost," yet they chose to remain silent about the issue.

While we are able to discern some of the names of the prominent members of the first con, the same cannot be said of Rogers's second group. After the fact, the only name that does appear in various accounts is one Alexander Carmichael, whose house Ransford visited the night he was caught. The name comes up only once, and it does so in a more recent account of the case; as such, it cannot be corroborated with any of the original sources.[114] What we do find about Mr. Carmichael is the fact that he was a one-time lieutenant in the Continental army. He married Mary Ogden, a daughter

The Presbyterian church today. This photograph was taken from the Morristown Green.
Photograph by the author.

of a prominent local family, and settled into his law practice after the war. If he was the one whose house Rogers visited while drunk, it would have been on Mary Ogden's hunch of misdeeds that led to Ransford's con being uncovered. As for the reverend to whom she brought the magic dust, all accounts point to it having been Reverend Timothy Johns, who was in charge of the Presbyterian Church in Morristown, where many members of the Company were recruited. This was before the completion of the newer church building, which the congregation moved into in 1791. Reverend Johns also corresponds with a Reverend T——— L———, as referenced in a story of the Morristown Ghost that was retold in the *Proceedings of the New Jersey Historical Society* 4 (1875–77).

⊷————⊷

Before Andrew Sherman published his *Historic Morristown, New Jersey: The Story of Its First Century* in one volume in 1905, he first published its contents serially in the Saturday issues of the *Newark Evening News*. As the separate chapters began appearing in the paper and it was becoming evident that, chronologically speaking, Sherman was going to cover the period of the Morristown Ghost, he received a letter from a follower of his weekly column. After expressing the pleasure with which he had been reading the story thus far, the man asked the author, "When you come to deal with the 'Morristown Ghost'…please let me know if you learn the names of the persons that were duped." In his response, Sherman kindly thanked the man for supporting his endeavor of writing the early history of the county but not before he admitted to having in his possession "the names" of all the fathers swindled by the Morristown Ghost. However, to the dismay of the inquisitive gentleman, he added that for the sake of the living descendants of those duped fathers, he did not consider it kind to publish them in his story of Morristown's first century.

> *"Why not?" Have several friends in manifest astonishment inquired of the writer, when he has expressed the disinclination to do so; "Why not; it is matter of history, is it not?"*

Opposite: The Presbyterian Church in Morristown, circa 1795. This building took over for the original church that stood during the original con. *Courtesy of the Morris County Historical Society.*

Right: Morris County historian Andrew M. Sherman, the author of *Historic Morristown, New Jersey. Courtesy of the Morris County Historical Society.*

> *Matter of history it most assuredly is, but this kind of argument is a two-edged sword that cleaves two ways. Because it is history and not myth or legend is a most potent reason, as the writer conceives why he should not publish the names of our worthy sires, the victims of superstitions, and* [perhaps] *of the misfortunes of was by which some of them were impoverished and hence made hypersensitive to the glitter of gold.*[115]

So even after more one hundred years, historians still protected the secret of Ransford Rogers's Company, or "Spirit Batch," as some accounts later called them. Perhaps they were right to do so at the time. But then again, is time not the greatest healer and forgiver of past errors and ills?

EPILOGUE

The story of the Morristown Ghost is as relevant today as it was at the time of its first publication in 1792. It is not a ghost tale—far from it. As history has shown, there is context to every story, a reason or a motivation for every human decision and their subsequent action. The people of late eighteenth-century Morris County who managed to get swindled were not merely gullible, they were products of their time. Who knows, maybe we would have done the same if we had lived with similar circumstances.

———◆————▶———

How exactly does one go about writing a ghost story that does not have a ghost? How does one write a true story involving real people without knowing who the people were? I guess we might as well ask how does one write history? When we type "Morristown Ghost" into Google, it will take approximately 0.44 seconds to be graced with 4,080,000 results. Colonel Benoni Hathaway comes back with a healthy 1,960,000 in the same record time—a testament to the caliber of a person the Revolutionary War hero was during his life. The number is again cut into more than half when searching David Carmichael, with 67,300 results. And when one searches one of the main places where the secret and ghostly meetings took place, namely Solitude in Morristown, the results drop down to 10, all of them pertaining to some current place and/or event, not the place in Morris

County in late 1700s. All of these present certain challenges to the historian conducting their research. What is significant and what is not? What should be talked about and what should be avoided? And finally, should things of the past stay in the past, or should we drag them out, dust them off, restore what is there, add what is missing and bring the whole back to relevance?

A presentation by a historian sponsored by the Washington Township Historical Society from 2014 enticed people to come hear the telling of "one of Morris County's funniest history stories of the eighteenth century."[116] Maybe *funny* is not the right word, yet one must commend the historical society for at least acknowledging that this event was history. The book you hold in your hand is an attempt at historical detection, looking for evidence and putting pieces together to form a new whole, answering old questions and asking new ones. Why would the most prominent and respected men of a county believe in a ghost story? Why would the existence of a hidden treasure be feasible? Who was Ransford Rogers, the only name left to us by history? Who were those involved, and why were their names suppressed? And finally, where did all these events take place? These questions and more became the focal point of this research, all behind the biggest mystery of it all—the 1792 pamphlet detailing the story. This work does not claim to be the all-encompassing history or even research on the topic. Perhaps calling it an introduction into historical detection would be more fitting.

The year prior to the publication of the original pamphlet, which was subsequently bought out and destroyed by the families of those involved, there appeared in the *New Jersey Journal* (Elizabethtown) on October 19, 1791, the following advertisement:

> *Friday evening next, at the Academy in this Town, will be presented: A Dramatic Peace, called* The Morris-Town Ghost; Or, The Force of Credulity; *to which will be added,* Chrononhotonthologos. *Tickets at three shillings each, to be had at Mr. Shute's. Doors to be opened at five o'clock, and the entertainment to begin precisely at six.*[117]

According to Sherman's *Historic Morristown*, the play was said to have been written by a son of Reverend James Richards, DD, a former Morristown pastor. It was acknowledged that the drama script was written directly for the occasion, and there is no trace of it ever being printed. Concurrently, no actors' notes survive. Still, if not for anything else, we are informed that the story of Rogers's scam in Morristown and its vicinity "was 'in the air' before it was 'in a book,'" which is, presumptively, at least, in favor of the authenticity of the story as graphically related in the volume of which every copy, so far as possible, was 'bought up and destroyed,' after its publication."[118]

Today, David Young's 1826 version of the pamphlet, titled *The Wonderful History of the Morristown Ghost; Thoroughly and Carefully Revised* is considered very rare. A quick eBay search at the time of this writing does yield a single copy for sale, with a starting bid of $250. Yet when attempting to purchase "the original" 1792 pamphlet of the story of the "Morristown Ghost," one would consider themselves lucky to just get the 1876 *Fac-Simile Copy* of the original, which sold for $1 at the time of its release. As for the original copy, the one said to presumably contain the real names of people and places involved in the scam—it still eludes today's collectors. That is not to say that it does not exist. Historian Andrew M. Sherman claimed to have held the original copy in his hands when conducting research for his 1905 *Historic Morristown*. "A careful comparison of the typography of this book with that of *The Prompter; or a Commentary on Common Sayings & Subject*, printed at Newark, New Jersey, in the year 1793 by John Woods, proves, to the satisfaction of the writer, that both books were printed at the same office."[119]

There is no doubt that the pamphlet existed. There can also be no doubt about the fact that the events described within its pages are real. The incident surrounding of the Morristown Ghost was not the first time people allowed themselves to get conned, and it most certainly will not be the last. As history proves to us again and again, anything is possible. After all, we may all be susceptible, at one time or another, to believe things that would normally not seem plausible. Anyone can be scammed—albeit today, it might come through an email, a text or a phone call, not in the form of ghostly apparition. So next time someone promises you easy riches, think of the story of the Morristown Ghost, or rather, one Ransford Rogers and his great Morris County con of 1788.

NOTES

Preface

1. James West Davidson and Mark Hamilton Lytle, *After the Fact: The Art of Historical Detection* (New York: Alfred A. Knopf, 1982), v.
2. Edward Hallett Carr, *What Is History?: The George Macaulay Trevelyan Lectures Delivered in the University of Cambridge January–March 1961*, second edition (New York: Penguin Books, 1987), 7–13, http://abuss.narod.ru/Biblio/eng/carr.pdf.
3. Ibid.
4. Ibid.
5. Ibid.
6. Ibid.
7. Pinelands Preservation Alliance, "The Jersey Devil and Folklore," https://pinelandsalliance.org/learn-about-the-pinelands/pinelands-history-and-culture/the-jersey-devil-and-folklore/.

Introduction

8. Dorianne R. Perrucci, *Morris County: The Progress of Its Legend* (Woodland Hills, CA: Windsor Publications, 1983), 34.
9. *Pennsylvania Gazette*, "A Witch Trial at Mount Holly," October 22, 1730, https://founders.archives.gov/documents/Franklin/01-01-02-0056.

10. George Washington's Mount Vernon, "Colonial Superstitions," https://www.mountvernon.org/blog/2018/10/colonial-superstitions.

11. Ibid.

12. Emil Frankel, "Crime Treatment in New Jersey: 1668–1934," *Journal of Criminal Law and Criminology* 28, no. 1 (May–June 1937): 4–6.

13. Ibid., 92.

14. Washington Township Public Schools, "Crime and Punishment in Colonial America," https://www.wtps.org/cms/lib/NJ01912980/Centricity/Domain/745/crime%20and%20punishment%20in%20coloial%20america.pdf.

Chapter 1

15. *Account of the Beginning, Transactions, and Discovery*, 16.

Chapter 2

16. Honeyman, *Northwestern New Jersey*, 387.

17. *Account of the Beginning, Transactions, and Discovery*, 22.

18. Honeyman, *Northwestern New Jersey*, 387.

19. Undine, "The Morristown Ghost; or Beware of Goblins Bearing Gifts," *Strange Company*, March 23, 2015, http://strangeco.blogspot.com/2015/03/the-morristown-ghost-or-beware-of.html.

Chapter 4

20. Nicholas Collin and Amadeus Johnson, "The Reverend Nicholas Collin on the Ravages of War," in *The Journal and Biography of Nicholas Collin, 1746–1831* (N.p.: New Jersey Society of Pennsylvania, 1936), n.p., https://dspace.njstatelib.org/xmlui/handle/10929/18632.

21. McCormick, *New Jersey from Colony to State*, 154.

22. Dennis P. Ryan, *New Jersey's Loyalists* (Trenton: New Jersey Historical Commission), 6, https://dspace.njstatelib.org/xmlui/bitstream/handle/10929/18670/h6731975e_v20.pdf?sequence=4.

23. Richard T. Irwin, *American Loyalists in Morris County* (Madison: Historiographers of New Jersey, 1996), 186–87.

24. Ibid., 176–79.
25. Joseph F. Tuttle, DD, "The Morristown Ghost," *Historical Magazine* 1, third series (January 1872): 2–10.
26. Delaware, Lackawanna and Western Railroad Company, *Mountain and Lake Resorts* (N.p.: Passenger Department, 1903), 54–57, https://books.google.com/books?id=L7hLAQAAIAAJ&pg=PA42&dq=Schooley+Mountain&hl=en&newbks=1&newbks_redir=1&sa=X&ved=2ahUKEwiNnbCGjNjsAhWRY98KHTo2A7MQ6AEwCXoECAQQAg#v=onepage&q=Schooley%20Mountain&f=false.
27. Washington Township, https://www.wtmorris.org/index.php.
28. Lewis F. Owen, *The Revolutionary Struggle in New Jersey* (Trenton, NJ: New Jersey Historical Commission), 13, https://dspace.njstatelib.org/xmlui/bitstream/handle/10929/18666/h6731975e_v16.pdf?sequence=4.
29. Ibid.
30. Thomas Fleming, *The Forgotten Victory: The Battle for New Jersey, 1780* (New York: Reader's Digest Press, 1973), 80–81.
31. Ibid., 162.
32. Ibid., 175.
33. Stryker, "Documents," 245.
34. Ibid., 255.
35. Thomas Fleming, "Crossroads of the American Revolution," in *New Jersey in the American Revolution*, 7.
36. Leonard Lundin, *Cockpit of the Revolution*, 219.
37. Stryker, "Documents," 277.
38. Ibid., 271–72.
39. Fleming, "Crossroads," 8.
40. Lee, "Documents," 422.
41. Ibid., 283–84.
42. *New Jersey Gazette*, "General's Proclamation," January 21, 1778.

Chapter 5

43. Eric Foner, *Give Me Liberty*, 2nd ed. (New York: WW. Norton, 2009), 105.
44. John Demos, "Religion and Witchcraft in Colonial America," https://www.gilderlehrman.org/history-resources/videos/religion-and-witchcraft-colonial-america.
45. Foner, *Give Me Liberty*, 105.
46. *History of Morris County*, 128.

47. *Account of the Beginning, Transactions, and Discovery*, 7.

48. John T. Cunningham, *New Jersey: A Mirror on America* (Florham Park, NJ: Afton Publishing, 1978), 77.

49. Ibid.

50. Ibid.

51. Ibid.

52. Tuttle, "Morristown Ghost," 2–10.

53. Ibid.

54. Ibid.

55. Ibid.

56. Frank R. Stockton, *Stories of New Jersey* (New Brunswick, NJ: Rutgers University Press, 1961), 193–94.

57. *Pennsylvania Gazette*, "Witch Trial at Mount Holly."

58. Ibid.

59. *Account of the Beginning, Transactions, and Discovery*, 7–8.

60. Ibid.

61. John L. Brooke, *The Refiner's Fire: The Making of Mormon Cosmology, 1644–1844* (Cambridge, UK: Cambridge University Press, 1994), 124.

62. Tuttle, "Morristown Ghost," 2–10.

63. Monica Witkowski and Caitlin Newman, "Witchcraft in Colonial Virginia," *Encyclopedia Virginia*, Virginia Humanities, December 7, 2020, https://www.encyclopediavirginia.org/witchcraft_in_colonial_virginia.

64. Stockton, *Stories of New Jersey*, 193.

65. Jon M. Shepard, *Sociology and You* (New York: McGraw Hill, 2003), 83.

66. Patrick Richard McCormick, *New Jersey: A Student's Guide to Localized History* (New York: Bureau of Publications, Teachers College, 1965), 7.

67. Davidson and Lytle, *After the Fact*, 35.

68. Ibid., 39.

69. Ibid., 41.

70. Ibid., 42.

71. Ibid.

Chapter 6

72. *History of Morris County*, 111.

73. Ibid.

74. Ibid.

75. Ibid.

76. Ibid.
77. Joseph F. Tuttle, DD, "The Early History of Morris County, New Jersey," New Jersey Roots, http://www.nj-roots.org/index.php/counties/morris-county/6-early-history-of-morris-county-new-jersey.
78. Ibid.
79. Ibid.
80. Ibid.
81. *History of Morris County*, 112.
82. Ibid.
83. *The Proceedings of the New Jersey Historical Society*, second series, vol. 4., *1875–1877* (Newark, NJ: Printed at the Daily Advertiser Office, 1877), 156.
84. *Pennsylvania Gazette*, "New York, September 24," September 29, 1773, 2.
85. Ibid.
86. Tuttle, "Early History of Morris County."
87. *History of Morris County*, 112.
88. *Pennsylvania Gazette*, "New York, September 24," 2.
89. *History of Morris County*, 112.
90. Brooke, *Refiner's Fire*, 124.
91. Ibid.

Chapter 7

92. Mappen, *Jerseyana*, 55.
93. Ibid.
94. Brooke, *Refiner's Fire*, 53–54.
95. Allegra di Bonaventura, *For Adam's Sake: A Family Saga in Colonial New England* (New York: Liveright Publishing Corporation, 2013), 31.
96. Ibid.
97. Tuttle, "Morristown Ghost," 2–10.
98. An account by the honorable Judge John Joseph Henry from the notes taken at the trial of one John Dady, published in the *Lancaster* (PA) *Examiner*, October 9, 1912, 6.
99. Ibid.
100. Ibid.
101. Ibid.

Chapter 8

102. Edwin S.S. Sunderland, *Old Wheatsheaf Farm, Formerly "Solitude", 1737; Prior to, During and Subsequent to the Continental Army and Washington's Headquarters Being Located, 1779–80 at Morristown New Jersey* (Old Wheatsheaf Farm, NJ: Pandick Press, October 21, 1955), 6.
103. Ibid.
104. U.S. Department of the Interior, Bureau of Land Management, "John Cleves Symmes," https://storymaps.arcgis.com/stories/68d80db184c54 13ca95a311310e72e1d.
105. Tuttle, "Morristown Ghost," 2–10.
106. Ibid.
107. Ruth Keightley, "Re: Benoni Hathaway NJ militia Rev War," Genealogy. com, August 11, 2002, https://www.genealogy.com/forum/surnames/ topics/hathaway/1896/.
108. Scott Shepherd, "Hathaway and Fairchild," N. California Settlers, https://cafamilies.org/gard/hath-frchld.html.
109. John Cresseveur, "The Hathaway Family," NJGenWeb, http://www. usgenwebsites.org/NJMorris/biographies/rockawayrecords/hathaway.htm.
110. Ibid.
111. Tuttle, "The Morristown Ghost," 2–10.
112. John Cresseveur, "The Lamson Family," NJGenWeb, http://www. usgenwebsites.org/NJMorris/biographies/rockawayrecords/lamson.htm.
113. Tuttle, "Morristown Ghost," 2–10.
114. Undine, "Morristown Ghost; or Beware of Goblins."
115. Andrew M. Sherman, *Historic Morristown, New Jersey: The Story of its First Century* (Morristown, NJ: Howard Publishing Company, 1905), 405–20.

Epilogue

116. Eileen Stokes, "Ransford Rogers, The Morristown Ghost and Schooley's Mountain's Treasure," Patch, https://patch.com/new-jersey/longvalley/ ransford-rogers-the-morristown-ghost-and--schooleys-mountains-treasure.
117. Andrew M. Sherman, *Historic Morristown*, 410.
118. Ibid.
119. Ibid.

SELECTED BIBLIOGRAPHY

An Account of the Beginning, Transactions and Discovery, of Ransford Rogers Who Seduced Many by Pretended Hobgoblins and Apparitions, and Thereby Extorted Money from Their Pockets: In the County of Morris and State of New-Jersey, in the Year 1788. Newark, NJ: Reproduced and for sale by L.A. Vogt, "Banner" Office, 1876.

Beck, Henry Charlton. *The Roads of Home: Lanes and Legends of New Jersey.* New Brunswick, NJ: Rutgers University Press, 1983.

————. *Tales and Towns of Northern New Jersey.* New Brunswick, NJ: Rutgers University Press, 1994.

Benvenuti, Judi, and Mary Ann Cataldo. *Morristown, the War Years, 1775–1783: Being a Pictorial History of the Area during the War of Independence, Depicting the Daily Activities, Recreation & Hardships of the Inhabitants and Soldiers, with Dialogue Furnished by the Participants.* Fort Washington, PA: Published for Morristown National Historical Park by Eastern National Park & Monument Association, 1979.

Bill, Alfred Hoyt. *New Jersey and the Revolutionary War.* New Brunswick, NJ: Rutgers University Press, 1972.

Casterline, Greg. *Colonial Tribulations: The Survival Story of William Casterline and His Comrades of the New Jersey Blues Regiment, French and Indian War, 1755–1757.* Morrisville, NC: Lulu Publishing, 2007.

Cohen, David Steven. *Folklore and Folklife of New Jersey.* New Brunswick, NJ: Rutgers University Press, 1983.

Cunningham, John T. *This Is New Jersey.* New Brunswick, NJ: Rutgers University Press, 1994.

Cunningham, John T., and Homer Hill. *New Jersey: America's Main Road.* New York: Doubleday, 1976.

Derry, Ellis L. *Old and Historic Churches of New Jersey*. Medford, NJ: Plexus Publishing, 1994.

Fleming, Thomas J. *New Jersey: A History*. Mountain View, CA: Norton, 1984.

Fowler, Alex D. *Splinters from the Past: Discovering History in Old Houses*. Morristown, NJ: Morris County Historical Society, 1984.

Gerlach, Larry R. *New Jersey's Revolutionary Experience*. Trenton, NJ: New Jersey Historical Commission, 1976.

History of Morris County, New Jersey, 1739–1882: With Illustrations and Biographical Sketches of Prominent Citizens and Pioneers. New York: W.W. Munsell & Co., 1882.

Hoffman, Robert Van Amburgh. *The Revolutionary Scene in New Jersey*. New York: American Historical Co., 1942.

Honeyman, A. Van Doren. *Northwestern New Jersey: A History of Somerset, Morris, Hunterdon, Warren and Sussex Counties*. Salem, MA: Higginson Book Company, 1997.

Hoskins, Barbara. *Men from Morris County, New Jersey, Who Served in the American Revolution*. Morristown, NJ: Friends of the Joint Free Public Library of Morristown and Morris Township, 1979.

Hull, Joan C. *Teacher's Guide for New Jersey: A Mirror on America*. Edina, MN: Afton Press, 1978.

Lundin, Leonard. *Cockpit of the Revolution*. Princeton, NJ: Princeton University Press, 1940.

Lurie, Maxine N., Marc Mappen and Maria M. Gillan. *Encyclopedia of New Jersey*. New Brunswick, NJ: Rutgers University Press, 2004.

MacCormick, Richard P. *New Jersey from Colony to State: 1609–1789*. New Brunswick, NJ: Rutgers University Press, 1964.

Mappen, Marc. *Jerseyana: The Underside of New Jersey History*. New Brunswick, NJ: Rutgers University Press, 1992.

McCormick, Richard P. *Experiment in Independence: New Jersey in the Critical Period 1781–1789*. New Brunswick, NJ: Rutgers University Press, 1950.

Mitnick, Barbara J., ed. *New Jersey in the American Revolution*. Newark, NJ: Rivergate Books, 2005.

Perrucci, Dorianne R., and Robert G. Geelan. *Morris County, the Progress of Its Legend*. Albany, NY: Windsor Publications, 1983.

Platt, Charles Davis. *Ballads of New Jersey in the Revolution*. Morristown, NJ: Kennikat Press, 1972.

Pomfret, John E. *The New Jersey Proprietors and Their Lands*. New York: Van Nostrand, 1964.

Salter, Edwin. *New Jersey Loyalists*. N.p.: n.p., 1884.

Stories of New Jersey: Its Significant Places, People and Activities, Compiled and Written by the Federal Writers' Project. New York: M. Barrows and Co., 1938.

Stryker-Rodda, Harriet. *Some Early Records of Morris County, New Jersey 1740–1799*. New York: Polyanthos, 1975.

Studley, Miriam Van Arsdale. *Historic New Jersey through Visitors' Eyes*. Princeton, NJ: D. Van Nostrand Company, 1964.

Thayer, Theodore. *Colonial and Revolutionary Morris County*. Whippany, NJ: Morris County Heritage Commission, 1975.

Weiss, Harry B. *Life in Early New Jersey*. New York: Van Nostrand, 1964.

State Archives and Digital Collections

Gerlach, Larry R., ed. "New Jersey in the American Revolution 1763 to 1783: A Documentary History." New Jersey Digital Collection of the American Revolution. https://www.njstatelib.org/research_library/new_jersey_resources/highlights/american_revolution/.

Lee, Francis B., ed. "Documents Relating to the Revolutionary History of the State of New Jersey." In *Archives of the State of New Jersey*. Second series. Vol. 2. Trenton, NJ: State Gazette Publishing Co. Printers, 1903.

Nelson, William, ed. "Documents Relating to the Revolutionary History of the State of New Jersey." In *Archives of the State of New Jersey*. Second series. Vol. 3. Trenton, NJ: State Gazette Publishing Co. Printers, 1906.

———. "Documents Relating to the Revolutionary History of the State of New Jersey." In *Archives of the State of New Jersey*. Second series. Vol. 4. Trenton, NJ: State Gazette Publishing Co. Printers, 1914.

———. "Documents Relating to the Revolutionary History of the State of New Jersey." In *Archives of the State of New Jersey*. Second series. Vol. 5. Trenton, NJ: State Gazette Publishing Co. Printers, 1916.

Stryker, William S., ed. "Documents Relating to the Revolutionary History of the State of New Jersey." In *Archives of the State of New Jersey*. Second series. Vol. 1. Trenton, NJ: State Gazette Publishing Co. Printers, 1901.

ABOUT THE AUTHOR

Peter Zablocki is a historian, educator and author of numerous books detailing New Jersey's history. His articles often appear in various popular history publications, and his podcast, *History Teachers Talking*, is available on all popular streaming platforms. For more information about his books, podcast or any upcoming events, visit www.peterzablocki.com.